Big Data Analytics for Risk and Insurance

Big Data Analytics for Risk and Insurance

Edited by

Michael W. Elliott, CPCU, ARM, AIAF, MBA

2nd Edition • 2nd Printing

The Institutes
720 Providence Road, Suite 100
Malvern, Pennsylvania 19355-3433

2nd Edition • 2nd Printing • June 2019

Library of Congress Control Number: 2018937940

ISBN 978-0-89462-218-2

Foreword

The Institutes are the knowledge partner that best provides educational activities related to risk management and property-casualty insurance, thereby empowering risk management and insurance professionals to help those in need. For more than 100 years, The Institutes have been meeting the public's changing insurance needs with customer-driven products and services.

In conjunction with outside experts and members of the academic community, our in-house professionals develop our course and program content, including Institutes study materials. Practical and technical knowledge gained from Institutes courses enhances qualifications, improves performance, and contributes to professional growth—all of which drive results.

The Institutes' proven knowledge helps individuals and organizations achieve powerful results with a variety of flexible, customer-focused options:

Recognized Credentials—The Institutes offer an unmatched range of widely recognized specialty credentials. Our flagship CPCU® designation provides learners with a broad understanding of the property-casualty insurance industry. Depending on their needs, CPCU students may select either a commercial insurance focus or a personal risk management and insurance focus and may choose from a variety of electives.

In addition, The Institutes offer certificate and designation programs in a variety of disciplines and on diverse topics, including these:

- Agent-broker
- Claims
- Commercial underwriting
- Cyber
- Fidelity and surety bonding
- General insurance
- Insurance accounting and finance
- Insurance information technology
- Insurance production and agency management
- Insurance regulation and compliance
- Management
- Marine insurance
- Personal insurance
- Premium auditing
- Quality insurance services
- Reinsurance
- Risk management
- Surplus lines

Ethics—Ethical behavior is crucial to preserving not only the trust on which insurance transactions are based but also the public's trust overall. All Institutes designations have an ethics requirement, which is delivered online and free of charge. Our ethics content relates to insurance issues and presents insurance-based case studies to outline an ethical framework.

Flexible Online Learning—The Institutes have an unmatched variety of technical insurance content covering topics from accounting to underwriting, which we now deliver through hundreds of online courses. These cost-effective self-study courses are a convenient way to fill gaps in technical knowledge in a matter of hours without ever leaving the office.

Continuing Education—A majority of The Institutes' courses are filed for CE credit in most states. We also deliver quality, affordable online CE courses quickly and conveniently through CEU. Visit CEU.com to learn more. CEU is powered by The Institutes.

College Credits—Most Institutes courses carry college credit recommendations from the American Council on Education. A variety of courses also qualify for credits toward certain associate, bachelor's, and master's degrees at several prestigious colleges and universities.

Custom Applications—The Institutes collaborate with corporate customers to use our trusted course content and flexible delivery options in developing customized solutions that help them achieve their unique organizational goals.

Insightful Analysis—Our Insurance Research Council (IRC) division conducts public policy research on important contemporary issues in property-casualty insurance and risk management. Visit www.Insurance-Research.org to learn more or purchase the IRC's most recent studies.

The Institutes look forward to serving the public through exemplary risk management and property-casualty insurance education solutions for another 100 years. In pursuit of this goal, we welcome your feedback, which helps us continually improve the quality of our study materials.

Peter L. Miller, CPCU
President and CEO
The Institutes

Preface

Big Data Analytics for Risk and Insurance is the assigned textbook for the AIDA 181 course in The Institutes' Associate in Insurance Data Analytics (AIDA) designation program. This course provides an overview of the application of advanced analytics to risk management and property-casualty insurance.

For many decades, risk managers and insurance professionals have employed conventional statistical techniques to support decision making in areas such as risk assessment, underwriting, and claims. However, the techniques employed by these professionals are quickly evolving, given the advent of big data and increasingly powerful data storage and processing capabilities. These developments have created opportunities for enhanced data-driven decision making, which can lead to superior business results.

Risk management, underwriting, and claims professionals who need a fundamental understanding of analytical techniques for big data will benefit from this course. It is also likely to benefit senior executives, data managers, and regulators who need knowledge of modern analytics to carry out their duties. The course is written for a nonquantitative audience and, to the extent possible, avoids using mathematical formulas when explaining analytical terminology and concepts.

Assignment 1 describes modern analytics, the influence of big data, and the commercialization of new technologies for internet-connected products—which make up the Internet of Things. This assignment also explores the roles of the data scientist and the actuary, along with the benefits of data mining and data-driven decision making.

Assignment 2 covers predictive modeling concepts, such as supervised and unsupervised learning, entropy, and lift. It also explains how to train a predictive model and evaluate its outputs. These concepts are used throughout subsequent assignments.

Assignment 3 explores traditional techniques for analyzing big data, including clustering, classification, and regression, while Assignment 4 explores the newer techniques of text mining, social network analysis, and neural networks. The application of these techniques is illustrated through risk management and insurance examples.

Assignment 5 reviews emerging technologies, such as artificial intelligence, wireless sensor networks, and computer vision and explains how they generate big data in support of underwriting, claims, and risk management.

Assignments 6 through 8 apply the previously introduced technologies and techniques to underwriting, focusing on ratemaking, pricing, and risk selection; claims fraud, claims assignment, and claims processes; and risk management, including risk identification and risk assessment.

Assignment 9 discusses data analytics from an organizational perspective. It covers the development of a data analytics strategy, along with the application of both the enterprise risk management process and the change management process to the implementation of advanced analytics throughout an organization.

This course illustrates some of the more common applications of data analytics. New uses for advanced analytics in underwriting, claims, and risk management will continue to be developed, increasing operating efficiency for insurance companies and benefiting their customers.

The Institutes are grateful for the guidance provided by the following individuals in the initial stages of course development: Mike Fitzgerald, CPCU, PMP; Erik F. Miller, MBA, CPCU, ARM, PMP, MSPA; and Stuart Rose.

For more information about The Institutes' programs, please call our Customer Success Department at (800) 644-2101, email us at CustomerSuccess@TheInstitutes.org, or visit our website at TheInstitutes.org.

Michael W. Elliott

Contributors

The Institutes acknowledge with deep appreciation the contributions made to the content of this text by the following persons:

Doug Froggatt, CPCU, AINS

Beth Illian, CPCU, AINS, AIS

Ann E. Myhr, CPCU, ARM, AU, AIM, ASLI

Contents

Direct Your Learning

1

Exploring Big Data Analytics

Educational Objectives

After learning the content of this assignment, you should be able to:

- Describe the evolution of big data and technology and its impact on the property-casualty insurance business.
- Categorize the various characteristics and sources of big data available for insurance and risk management applications.
- Summarize these aspects of data quality:
  - The concept of data quality
  - Basic techniques to improve data quality
- Describe data mining and the data mining process.
- Explain how data science applies to risk management and insurance and the role of the data scientist.
- Explain how data-driven decision making applies to risk management and insurance.

Outline

Exploring Big Data Analytics

1

BIG DATA AND TECHNOLOGY—THE FUTURE OF INSURANCE

Technology has transformed our lives in how we communicate, learn, and do business. It also continues to evolve at a rapid pace. For example, self-driving cars, once thought to be a subject of science fiction, are now a reality. Technology has already changed the insurance industry, and these changes have only just begun. The convergence of **big data** and technology has started a transformation of the property-casualty insurance business.

Big data

Sets of data that are too large to be gathered and analyzed by traditional methods.

Insurance would not be feasible without data. The ability of insurers to provide coverage for a variety of risk exposures is based on the **law of large numbers.** Traditionally, the data insurers use has come from loss histories. By analyzing large numbers of claims, insurers could reasonably predict the probable cost of future claims.

Law of large numbers

A mathematical principle stating that as the number of similar but independent exposure units increases, the relative accuracy of predictions about future outcomes (losses) also increases.

However, as technology evolves, the sources and amount of data available to insurers are increasing rapidly. To effectively use this data, insurers must continue to develop new methods of obtaining, processing, and analyzing it.

Strategic Opportunities From Big Data and Technology

Why would an insurance professional who is not an actuary or a data scientist want to learn about data analytics? The most comprehensive reason is that big data and technology are central to the future of the insurance industry. The evolution of this area has already disrupted the traditional ways in which insurers market, underwrite, and analyze their products. This disruption will only gain momentum with such changes on the horizon as self-driving cars, sensors in products ranging from bridges to jeans, and computers that teach themselves without human intervention.

Another, more practical reason is that insurance professionals, such as those in underwriting and claims, must be able to communicate with the data scientists in their organizations. Those who are engaged in the typical work of an insurer may serve on multifunctional teams to assist in the design of approaches to data analytics. Additionally, professionals in traditional insurance functions will need to understand how to use the techniques developed by data scientists to make decisions. Also, as the application of data analytics to insurance continues to evolve, professionals in areas such as underwriting and claims will be valuable in evaluating the results of the new techniques. Communication between those who perform the daily work of an insurer and those designing data analytics is important for success.

Data-driven decision making has been proved to produce better business results than other types of decision-making. For example, the credit industry was using data to select clients and determine credit lines. The data was obtained from loss histories, and the goal was to determine the probability of default. Signet Bank, a small bank, wanted to determine which potential clients would be profitable; however, it did not have that data available. Signet decided to accept a certain cost to obtain the data—the bank began providing credit randomly; losses increased significantly, and this was the cost of data acquisition. However, the data the bank acquired enabled its data scientists to develop predictive models that identified the characteristics of the most profitable clients. The bank then used the results to develop a strategy regarding which credit products to offer to which clients at what level of credit and interest rate. Signet Bank became Capital One.

Apply Your Knowledge

Why would claims, underwriting, or risk management professionals study data analytics?

a. To become data scientists

b. To be able to communicate with data scientists

c. To make high-level strategic decisions for their insurers

d. To learn how to design models to obtain data

Feedback: b. Claims or underwriting professionals typically study data analytics to be able to communicate with data scientists in their organizations. Although claims, underwriting, or risk management professionals may use the results of data analytics in their decision making, they would not usually make high-level decisions for insurers. They also would not be expected to become data scientists or to learn how to design models to obtain data.

Big Data

Although insurers have always gathered and analyzed large amounts of data to make business decisions, the amount of data available has increased exponentially and is therefore referred to as big data. Two types of big data are available to insurers. The first is their own internal data, and the second is data from external sources.

Why would insurers' own internal data now be considered advancements that require new methods of analysis? The answer is based on techniques such as **data mining** and **text mining**. An example of data mining is using a new technique to identify previously unknown factors that are common to an insurer's most profitable auto insurance customers. Other advanced techniques can enable innovative ways to market to those customers. Text mining can be used to analyze claims adjusters' notes to identify fraud indicators.

Data mining
The analysis of large amounts of data to find new relationships and patterns that will assist in developing business solutions.

Text mining
Obtaining information through language recognition.

New external sources of big data are constantly evolving. An example of an external source that some insurers are using is **telematics**. The data provided by telematics is analyzed to determine the driving patterns that lead to accidents as well as reflect safe driving. This information can result in a real-time change in premium if the auto owner agrees. A safe driver could receive a discount, while an unsafe driver may receive a premium increase and/or be required to attend a remedial driving program. The information obtained from telematics can also be applied to an insurer's online application and selection process.

Telematics
The use of technological devices in vehicles with wireless communication and GPS tracking that transmit data to businesses or government agencies; some return information for the driver.

Technology

Technology is constantly providing innovative products that are changing risk management and insurance. Similar to telematics devices, sensors can provide a stream of data to insurers regarding risk. Heat sensors can provide information about fire risk to both the customer and the insurer. Sensors on machinery can indicate a malfunction or the removal of a safety device. Sensors are now being included in clothing, which are referred to as wearables. Wearables in uniforms can provide valuable ergonomic information to improve safety.

An emerging area of technology is the **Internet of Things (IoT)**. Although this technology is still being explored for its potential in insurance, it is likely to evolve rapidly. The IoT is similar to telematics, home sensors, and wearable technology, but its potential is more extensive. The potential involves machine-to-machine communication and **machine learning**. The IoT may eventually be able to identify the next asbestos-type problem before it occurs by analyzing data from wearables, sensors, and text mining. For example, nanotechnology is a relatively new type of process, and its eventual effects are still unknown. The IoT could help insurers monitor risks associated with this process.

Internet of Things (IoT)
A network of objects that transmit data to computers.

Machine learning
Artificial intelligence in which computers continually teach themselves to make better decisions based on previous results and new data.

Drones are a new technological source of information, and they can produce data for underwriting or claims management. Instead of sending adjusters to a disaster scene, insurers are now testing the use of drones to provide detailed data about property damage. Drones, along with other technological tools such as cell phones and the Internet, can assist in gathering risk data for underwriting property coverage in wildfire-prone areas. Results from modeling data already obtained have provided the new, valuable insight that a well-constructed, well-maintained property in a high-risk area can be a better risk than a poorly maintained one in a moderate-risk area.

Social media is a rich source of data. Google and Facebook target advertisements to people who are likely to be interested in a particular product based on their profiles on social media sites. Google, Facebook, and Apple are also developing **artificial intelligence (AI)** to solve problems and introduce new products and services. For example, Google uses AI to find answers to rare search inquiries. All these organizations are researching techniques that will provide and analyze information from voice recordings, photos, and videos.

Artificial intelligence (AI)
Computer processing or output that simulates human reasoning or knowledge.

AI has significant potential for insurers. For example, claims adjusters often take recorded statements from claimants. AI techniques could be applied to recognize voice patterns that may indicate the possibility of fraud. There could also be applications related to photos of accidents or natural catastrophes. However, whether and to what extent insurers can use social media, such as videos posted on Facebook, is subject to regulatory and privacy concerns.

Data Science

Data science is a new field that arose from the need to link big data and technology in ways that provide useful knowledge. As discussed earlier, big data, by definition, is an amount of data too large to be analyzed by traditional methods. Data scientists have interdisciplinary skills in mathematics, statistics, computer programming, and sometimes engineering that allow them to perform data analytics on big data.

Data science
An interdisciplinary field involving the design and use of techniques to process very large amounts of data from a variety of sources and to provide knowledge based on the data.

Data scientists use various techniques to organize and analyze data. Machine learning is one example. Traditional techniques, such as probability, are often combined with newer techniques to obtain the most relevant knowledge from the data. A major concept in data science is that the data organization and analysis are automated rather than performed by an individual.

However, human evaluation of automated data analysis is critical. First, analysis performed by computers is not always accurate. An example is weather forecasting. Different models interpret meteorological data differently and produce varying forecasts. Experienced meteorologists must evaluate all of the model analyses and use their professional judgment to make a decision. Second, the automated analysis may be correct but irrelevant to a given business problem. For example, an automated analysis of claims information indicating that teenaged male drivers are more likely to have accidents would not be relevant to a deeper understanding of auto accident risk because the information about teenaged male drivers is already known. And third, just as technology is rapidly evolving, so are the physical, political, economic, and business environments. Unless the automated method can take those factors into account, the results of the automated analysis may not be helpful if the environment suddenly changes.

For data science to be useful to an insurer or to specific functional areas, such as underwriting or claims, it is usually important to define the business problem to be solved, such as improving claims or underwriting results. In the future, data analytics may be used to forecast unforeseen, or "black swan," events. However, this is still an area for exploration rather than application to business decisions.

Strategic Applications to Insurance

Insurers and risk managers should determine which investments in big data and technology will provide the best fit for their business. For example, an insurer that provides only personal lines of coverage may not be interested in wearables. A company that operates a fleet of vehicles may be more interested in telematics than building sensors. Insurers and risk managers also need to decide on the computers and software to process the increasing amounts of data.

After the data has been obtained and processed, insurance analytics must be applied to make data-driven decisions and develop strategy. This involves not only the big data, technology, and data science techniques but also people who can evaluate the results of the analytics.

Insurance professionals in areas such as underwriting, claims, and risk management should have input into the types of data that they know would be helpful to their decision making, such as fraud indicators. These professionals should also have input into how well the analytics are working to produce relevant and practical information or to improve efficiency.

At more senior levels of an insurer, the information obtained from data analytics can guide decisions such as which lines of coverage management wants to increase or decrease, countries where it would like to expand or reduce operations, and even investment decisions. See the exhibit "Process of Developing Strategy With Data Analytics."

Process of Developing Strategy With Data Analytics

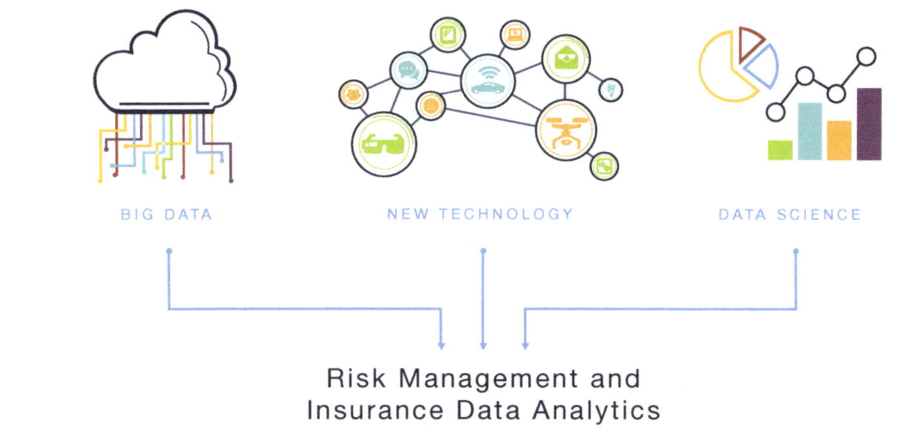

[DA11928]

Evolution of Big Data

Big data and technology can be regarded in stages of evolution. The first is Big Data 1.0, which is the stage at which many organizations are now. The next stage is Big Data 2.0. Some organizations are already at this stage. There will certainly be future stages as the technology continues to evolve.

Big Data 1.0

In Big Data 1.0, organizations began using the Internet to conduct business and compile data about their customers. Insurers developed online insurance applications. They also used the data from applications, as well as claims history, to improve underwriting efficiency and to provide customer information for product development and marketing.

Other industries were performing similar functions in Big Data 1.0. For example, retail investment firms, such as E*Trade, could use the Internet to provide new products to customers. Computers could place stock and bond trades much more efficiently than previous methods.

Big Data 2.0

Because of rapid advances in data science, we have reached the stage of Big Data 2.0. This stage allows organizations to obtain and aggregate vast amounts of data very quickly and extract useful knowledge from it.

For example, investment firms have computers that can scan the Internet instantly for news and information about products, prices, economic and geopolitical developments, and consumer trends. This data is then provided to computer trading algorithms that conduct automated trading of stocks and bonds at high speeds. Many people in the financial industry believe that computer trading has completely altered the world's major stock markets. There are questions regarding whether traditional forms of investing that individual investors use, such as selecting particular stocks, can be effective in the new trading environment of Big Data 2.0.

Big Data 2.0 also allows organizations to process and analyze data from sources such as vehicles, homes, and wearable technology. Sensors can be built into products, and data science provides methods to process and analyze the data that comes from those sensors. Big Data 2.0 is evolving quickly. Some insurers are already actively involved in this phase, while others are lagging. It is not an exaggeration to say that insurers that can adapt quickly and effectively to the convergence of big data and technology will have significant competitive advantages.

BIG DATA CHARACTERISTICS AND SOURCES

Insurers' traditional data is organized into databases with defined fields. Insurance professionals can produce reports that show results from this data. Risk managers can usually access their insurers' data to produce reports about claims they are handling. Big data has introduced different types and sources of data than those traditionally used.

It is important for risk management and insurance professionals to understand the different types of big data. The varieties, volume, and sources of data are rapidly increasing. For example, risk managers can obtain new types of data on safety from sources such as sensors on employees. Underwriters can obtain new data on risks from drones and social media. Claims adjusters can better identify fraud by identifying patterns in internal and external data. Risk management and insurance professionals increasingly work with data scientists to determine the types of data that are useful to make business decisions.

To better understand big data, these categories will be discussed:

- Data characteristics
- Internal and external data
- Structured and unstructured data

Data Characteristics

The term "big data" implies large quantities of data. Although this is true, big data is also different from traditional data in other respects.

These are characteristics that differentiate big data from traditional data:

- Volume—There is an enormous amount of data that is now available, and the amount continues to increase. To use an analogy, traditional data is like the planet earth, and big data is like the solar system. Eventually, big data could increase to the infinite size of the universe.
- Variety—Traditionally, insurers used **structured data**. Big data also includes structured data in larger volume than traditional data. However, because big data comes from multiple sources, much of it is **unstructured data**.
- Velocity—This is the constantly increasing speed at which data arrives at an insurer. Velocity also includes the growing rate of change in the types of data.
- Veracity—This refers to the completeness and accuracy of data. Unstructured big data is more likely to have less veracity than structured data. However, even traditional structured data will not be perfect. Also, insurers can often gain useful information from big data, even if it has lower veracity.
- Value—Value is derived from the results of data analysis to help insurers make better business decisions. Big data has great potential to add value, but it must be obtained and analyzed with techniques that provide meaningful results. This is the goal of data science.

Structured data
Data organized into databases with defined fields, including links between databases.

Unstructured data
Data that is not organized into predetermined formats, such as databases, and often consists of text, images, or other nontraditional media.

Internal and External Data

Data science allows insurers access to increasingly larger and more varied data, referred to as big data. Some of this data is received directly by the insurer or the risk manager's organization. Other data is obtained from outside sources.

Internal Data

Insurers have always relied on data, and they possess large quantities of it. Certain types of data, such as risk factors, losses, premium, rating factors, rates, and customer information, have been traditionally used to make business decisions. Much of this data is also reported to state rating bureaus. Similarly, risk managers also have relied on data about losses and premium, in addition to safety statistics that are reported to the Occupational Safety and Health Administration (OSHA).

Internal data
Data that is owned by an organization.

However, risk managers and insurers have vast quantities of **internal data** that they have not used because of its volume and/or a lack of techniques to access it. For example, an insurer may not analyze computer claims codes about claimants' preexisting medical conditions—traditional internal data that could be useful if data science techniques are applied to it.

Data science also provides techniques to use nontraditional internal data. For example, voice analysis can be applied to recorded statements of claimants to identify vocal characteristics associated with fraud, such as gaps in the claimant's version of the accident or a defensive tone. Underwriters often obtain photos of property, and claims adjusters often obtain photos of an accident scene. Artificial intelligence can analyze these photos to find information that may be missed by a human analysis, such as potential environmental hazards around a property or, through facial recognition, the identity of a witness to an accident.

External Data

External data
Data that belongs to an entity other than the organization that wishes to acquire and use it.

There is sometimes a blurring of the boundary between internal and **external data**. For example, data from telematics is obtained from a device that is installed on a customer's vehicle. The insurer owns the device, but the customer owns the vehicle. Because of the customer's ownership of the vehicle and the nature of the data provided—the customer's personal driving habits—telematics should probably be categorized as external data.

Another source of data with a blurred boundary is a wearable sensor used by an employee while working. The employer provides the sensor, but it is placed on the employee's person and transmits information about the individual. This information could be considered internal data because it is used in the workplace and because the sensor is owned by the employer. However, it could also be considered external data because it is obtained from and about an individual.

Other sources of external data include sensors in customers' homes or commercial buildings, photos of a catastrophe obtained by drones, and the Internet—especially social media. For insurers to access information from sensors on customers' property, customers must first grant permission. Regulators have already approved the use of drones by insurers to inspect catastrophe scenes. However, there may be other regulations governing what information can be used and how it can be used.

Privacy issues are a legal and regulatory concern in obtaining mass information from public sources, including social media. This is particularly true with data science because it is used to discover and analyze previously unknown data relationships. For example, an insurance company might access individual items of data on a claimant from both internal and external sources. While the data from each source by itself might not violate the claimant's privacy, combining all the data might lead to conclusions that harm the claimant's privacy in a way that he or she did not anticipate. As a result, privacy regulations have been passed by various states and countries. See the exhibit "The National Association of Insurance Commissioners' Insurance Consumer 'Cybersecurity Bill of Rights'."

Other sources of external data include statistical plan data, other aggregated insurance industry data, competitors' rate filings, and third-party data. The most commonly used types of third-party data are **economic data** and **geodemographic data**. Additionally, insurers obtain and use credit ratings for both personal and commercial lines of insurance where permitted by law.

Economic data

Data regarding interest rates, asset prices, exchange rates, the Consumer Price Index, and other information about the global, the national, or a regional economy.

Geodemographic data

Data regarding classifications of a population.

Structured and Unstructured Data

As mentioned above, data can be either structured or unstructured. The traditional data that insurers use for underwriting and claims management is structured. This data is organized into databases that are often linked to each other. For example, an underwriter could query one database regarding a customer's claims history and another database regarding the customer's premium history. The underwriter could receive this information in the same report because the databases are linked. Telematics provide an example of structured external data. There are predetermined fields in a database for the driving information that insurers receive from telematics, such as distance traveled, braking, and left turns.

Unstructured data is not organized. Adjusters' notes are an example of internal unstructured data. Although the notes are contained in individual claims files identified by numbers, there is no database that categorizes the data contained in the notes and provides results. Unstructured external data includes information from the Internet, such as social media.

Data science is used for both structured and unstructured data, but it is especially useful for unstructured data. Data scientists use various techniques to gather, categorize, and analyze unstructured data. This process may or may not produce useful results. For example, if an insurer is concerned about an

The National Association of Insurance Commissioners' Insurance Consumer 'Cybersecurity Bill of Rights'

As an insurance consumer, you have the right to:

1. Know the types of personal information collected and stored by your insurance company, agent or any business it contracts with (such as marketers and data warehouses).
2. Expect insurance companies/agencies to have a privacy policy posted on their websites and available in hard copy, if you ask. The privacy policy should explain what personal information they collect, what choices consumers have about their data, how consumers can see and change/correct their data if needed, how the data is stored/protected, and what consumers can do if the company/agency does not follow its privacy policy.
3. Expect your insurance company, agent or any business it contracts with to take reasonable steps to keep unauthorized persons from seeing, stealing or using your personal information.
4. Get a notice from your insurance company, agent or any business it contracts with if an unauthorized person has (or it seems likely he or she has) seen, stolen or used your personal information. This is called a data breach. This notice should:

- Be sent in writing by first-class mail or by e-mail if you have agreed to that.
- Be sent soon after a data breach and never more than 60 days after a data breach is discovered.
- Describe the type of information involved in a data breach and the steps you can take to protect yourself from identity theft or fraud.
- Describe the action(s) the insurance company, agent or business it contracts with has taken to keep your personal information safe.
- Include contact information for the three nationwide credit bureaus.
- Include contact information for the company or agent involved in a data breach.

5. Get at least one year of identity theft protection paid for by the company or agent involved in a data breach.
6. If someone steals your identity, you have a right to:

- Put a 90-day initial fraud alert on your credit reports. (The first credit bureau you contact will alert the other two.)
- Put a seven-year extended fraud alert on your credit reports.
- Put a credit freeze on your credit report.
- Get a free copy of your credit report from each credit bureau.
- Get fraudulent information related to the data breach removed (or "blocked") from your credit reports.
- Dispute fraudulent or wrong information on your credit reports.
- Stop creditors and debt collectors from reporting fraudulent accounts related to the data breach.
- Get copies of documents related to the identity theft.
- Stop a debt collector from contacting you.

"NAIC Roadmap for Cybersecurity Consumer Protection," National Association of Insurance Commissioners, 2015, www.naic.org/documents/committees_ex_cybersecurity_tf_related_roadmap_cybersecurity_consumer_protections.pdf (accessed March 7, 2015). [DA11943] increase in the frequency and severity of windstorm losses, it may want to gather data about weather patterns. Obtaining and analyzing unstructured information from news and weather reports on the Internet may provide a result the insurer already knows, namely that windstorms are increasing in frequency and severity. However, in another example, if an insurer wants to develop a more accurate profile of a claimant who commits insurance fraud, obtaining and analyzing unstructured internal data from adjusters' notes and external data from social media may provide information that can be used to develop a profile for claims investigations. See the exhibit "Big Data Categories and Examples."

Big Data Categories and Examples

	Structured	Unstructured
External	Telematics Financial data Labor statistics	Social media News reports Internet videos
Internal	Policy information Claims history Customer data	Adjuster notes Customer voice records Surveillance videos

[DA11944]

DATA QUALITY

The quality of data has always been important to insurers because inaccurate claims or underwriting data could have a significant financial effect. Big data and technology increase the volume, velocity, and variety of data—they therefore increase concerns about the quality of data as well.

Insurance and risk management professionals should understand the importance of data quality from two perspectives. The first is that of a data producer. Data producers—such as claims adjusters, underwriters, and risk managers—are often responsible for entering data into databases or reports, so they should be certain that the data they can control is as accurate and complete as possible. The second perspective is that of a data user. Users of data, such as the data in an accident report or application for insurance, need to be sure that it is of high quality. Also, professionals who use reports based on data, such as accident year loss costs for personal auto insurance, should be alert for any inconsistent results, such as reserves that appear too low or high, and report the discrepancy to the appropriate party.

Data Quality Defined

Quality data is accurate, appropriate, reasonable, and comprehensive relative to a given use. Accurate data is free from mistakes and can therefore be relied on to produce useful results.

Certain dimensions of data determine whether it is appropriate, such as its timeliness or historic value, the source from which the data was collected or derived, whether it is independent or depends on other appropriate data, and the likelihood that the data will produce a reliable result or assessment. Quality data should be free of any material limitations. If limitations exist, reasonable alternatives should be used if available. For example, when selecting data for a study to determine the number of auto accidents that occurred while the driver was texting, claims that occurred before 2005 would be materially limited because of the infrequency of texting before that year.

Reasonable data represents or is similar to other data (or knowledge) both within and outside the organization; in other words, it is internally and externally homogeneous. Reasonable data has been validated by comparison with outside sources or audited for consistency and accuracy. For example, data used to evaluate auto rates charged according to age must include age groupings that have been used consistently within the organization and in nationwide claims databases.

Comprehensive data contains the full range of information needed to produce a reliable result or analysis. Using the example of evaluating auto rates by age, all relevant claims data must be used, such as claim payments, settlement amounts, territory, type of claim (property damage or bodily injury), and causes of loss.

Insurers do not only use their data internally. They also submit various types of premium and claims data to the states in which they do business and to rating bureaus. Inaccurate data can therefore affect the results of the entire industry. Risk managers have a responsibility to ensure that data submitted to underwriters and claims adjusters is accurate. Inaccurate data from the source will have a ripple effect that could lead to costly consequences.

Metadata

Metadata documents the contents of a database. In addition to information about the data contained in the database, metadata contains information about business rules and data processing. An example of insurance metadata is a **statistical plan** created by a state regulatory agency or rating bureau.

The purpose of metadata is to make the information used by analysts as transparent as possible. This prevents any misunderstanding of the information that might lead to misuse or inaccurate conclusions.

Metadata
The data about data that provides context for analyzing transaction facts with efficient structures for grouping hierarchical information.

Statistical plan
A formal set of directions for recording and reporting insurance premiums, exposures, losses, and sometimes loss expenses to a statistical agent.

As an example, the metadata for a three-year compilation of accident year incurred losses should address these factors:

- The accident years included in the report
- The range of dates of paid loss transactions
- The evaluation date of the case-based loss reserve transactions
- The definition of incurred losses (such as paid plus latest loss reserve, inclusive or exclusive of allocated expenses, net of deductibles or reinsurance, and so forth)

Metadata can provide criteria for edits or restrictions of data inputs. A best practice is to reject, or at least flag, inputs that fail to meet the criteria. It is also useful to include a data quality matrix for each data element that describes the quality checks done on the data element, how frequently the checks are done, and where in the process the checks occur.

Metadata can be enhanced by process documentation. For example, a high-level data process flow diagram that shows each initial data source and the associated databases will give analysts better insight into the processing.

Methods to Identify Inaccurate or Missing Data

Quality can be compromised at many points in the data-collection process. These are examples of typical data quality problems:

- Missing data and null values, which impair or prevent an analyst's ability to use the affected variables (data elements) for analysis
- Data errors, such as coding a paid amount of $1,000 as $1 million or coding New York state (NY) as New Jersey (NJ)
- Default values rather than actual values (used by the person entering the data if the actual value is unknown)
- Duplicate transactions, such as entering the same claim or insurance application twice

Data takes two forms. One is quantitative, or numerical. The other is categorical, or alphanumeric. For example, $1,000 is quantitative, and NY is categorical. Different techniques are used to identify missing data or errors related to each of these forms.

Quantitative Data

Various techniques are used to identify missing or inaccurate quantitative data. One of these techniques is **descriptive statistics.** Statistical software can calculate characteristics such as mean, median, minimum, and maximum values and display that information in a table. For example, the descriptive statistics in the "Allocated Loss Adjustment Expenses" table summarize key information about the paid allocated expenses in the data. A review of the minimum and maximum values can quickly indicate whether any values

Descriptive statistics
Quantitative summaries of the characteristics of a dataset, such as the total or average.

appear to be outliers or have unusual values. In this example, the minimum paid expense is a negative value, and the second-smallest value is also negative. Both of these negative numbers indicate data records that should be reviewed further before being used for analysis. See the exhibit "Descriptive Statistics Related to Allocated Loss Adjustment Expenses."

Descriptive Statistics Related to Allocated Loss Adjustment Expenses

Allocated Loss Adjustment Expenses	
Mean	1,323
Standard Error	252
Median	611
Mode	0
Standard Deviation	8,217
Sample Variance	67,513,031
Minimum	(19)
Maximum	170,649
Sum	1,411,246
Count	1,067
Largest (2)	99,206
Smallest (2)	(11)

[DA11957]

Categorical Data

Data cube

A multidimensional partitioning of data into two or more categories.

Techniques, such as descriptive statistics, that are applied to quantitative data cannot be applied to categorical data; the data must be separated by category. Analysts typically use **data cubes** to divide the data into chunks, or groupings, and then see what is in the chunks. These chunks are then organized into tables that allow the data to be analyzed for unusual values. For example, an analyst wants to evaluate the effects of a new safety training program meant to reduce injuries to employees who drive delivery trucks. The injury types are those caused by vehicle accident, exertion/lifting while loading and unloading the trucks, and slips/falls while entering and exiting the trucks. The analyst wants to compare the injuries to drivers who have been through the training with those of drivers who have not. A data cube is used to determine the percentage of each combination of injury type and training in the accident data for the past year. See the exhibit "Table Displaying Percentage of Injuries by Training Category."

Table Displaying Percentage of Injuries by Training Category

	Vehicle Accident		Exertion/Lifting		Slip/Fall	
	Number	Percent	Number	Percent	Number	Percent
Training	31	5%	147	22%	83	13%
No Training	57	9%	205	31%	79	12%
Blank/Missing Data	7	1%	34	5%	8	2%

[DA12042]

There was a total of 651 claims in the designated injury categories. Because the accident/injury type field is required to process a claim, there was no missing data for the three causes of injury. However, the data fields for training are not required fields, and there are missing data elements in this category. The analyst will need to identify the missing data elements to accurately analyze the data.

Data Security

Data quality depends in part on the security of the data. Insurers must safeguard the accuracy of both their information systems and the data on which important decisions are based. Data may be inaccurate because of flaws in the system's ability to detect erroneous transactions or a lack of security. Additionally, without adequate controls, those with access to data may be able to change it.

A best practice is to restrict access to data. Authorized users' levels of access should be based on their responsibilities. For example, certain users may only retrieve data while others may have the authority to add, delete, or modify the data.

Insurers must also apply cyber security techniques to reduce the likelihood that **malware** will corrupt data in their systems. Additionally, proper cyber security reduces the probability that the data will be accessed by someone outside the organization, whose intention may be to not only obtain customer information but also fraudulently manipulate data.

Malware

Malicious software, such as a virus, that is transmitted from one computer to another to exploit system vulnerabilities in the targeted computer.

DATA MINING

Big data can be very useful to insurers and other organizations. However, it is only useful if it can be properly processed and analyzed.

Data mining is the application of various techniques to big data. Data mining and the data mining process allow organizations to analyze large amounts of internal and external data from various sources.

Data Mining Techniques

Statistics

A field of science that derives knowledge from data; it provides a root understanding of useful approaches to data analysis.

Database

A collection of information stored in discrete units for ease of retrieval, manipulation, combination, or other computer processing.

Data mining is closely related to the fields of **statistics**, machine learning, and **database** management.

Although data analysts use different approaches, depending on the nature of the data and the business problem, these are the basic techniques of data mining:

- Classification—Assigning members of a dataset into categories based on known characteristics. For example, an insurer wants to predict which insureds in its mid-size commercial lines of business are unlikely to renew their policies. Each insured could be classified as likely to renew or unlikely to renew based on specific characteristics, such as size, location, and types of coverage. The insurer could then develop solutions to increase renewals among those customers identified as unlikely to renew.
- Regression analysis—A statistical technique that predicts a numerical value given characteristics of each member of a dataset. For example, an insurer might want to learn the percentage of premium increase that would lessen a customer's likelihood of renewing an auto policy. By analyzing customers using the variables of nonrenewal and percentage of premium increase, the insurer could develop a regression model to analyze customers and provide a probability score.

Algorithm

An operational sequence used to solve mathematical problems and to create computer programs.

- Association rule learning—Examining data to discover new and interesting relationships. From these relationships, **algorithms** are used to develop rules to apply to new data. An insurer can explore data to find relationships among its products purchased. For example, through data mining, the insurer might discover that customers who purchase more than $250,000 in homeowners policy limits have a high probability of purchasing an umbrella policy. Rules for a computer program can then be developed to identify new customers who might be interested in purchasing both a homeowners and an umbrella policy.
- Cluster analysis—Using statistical methods, a computer program explores data to find groups with common and previously unknown characteristics. The results of the cluster analysis may or may not provide useful information. For example, an insurer may learn that drivers who watch more hours of television have more accidents, but this information is not likely to be useful to the insurer. However, cluster analysis may identify possibilities for new insurance products.

Classification and regression analysis are data mining techniques that are applied when an insurer knows what information it wants to predict. In the examples above, an insurer knows that it wants to predict which customers are unlikely to renew their policies or the probability that a customer will not renew if the premium is increased by a certain percentage. The insurer also knows the specific characteristics of the data it plans to analyze to find the answers to these questions. See the exhibit "Data Mining."

Data Mining

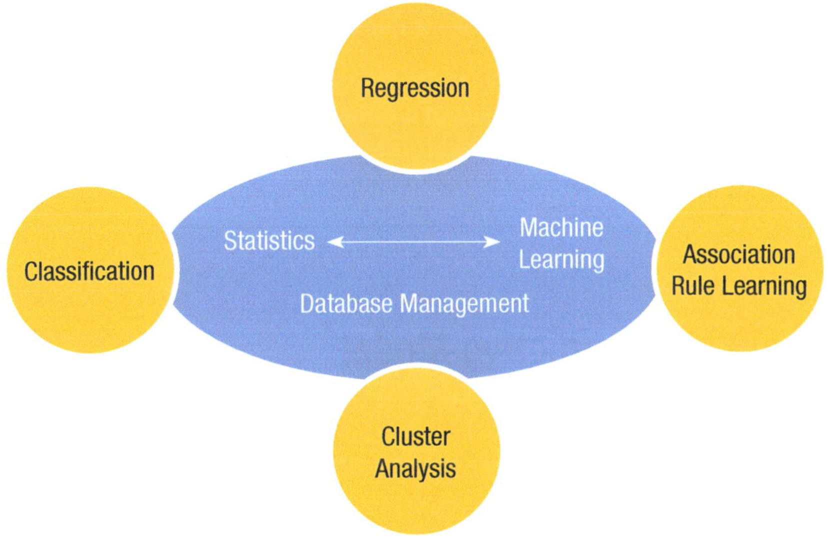

[DA11958]

Association rule learning and cluster analysis are used to explore data to make discoveries. Insurers, like other businesses, might apply cluster analysis to discover customer needs that could lead to new products. Unlike classification and regression analysis, there are no known characteristics of the data beforehand. The purpose of association rule learning and cluster analysis is to discover relationships and patterns in the data and then determine if that information is useful for making business decisions.

Apply Your Knowledge

An insurer wants to predict which claims may be fraudulent and target them for additional investigation. It wishes to do this based on the known fraud indicators of a claimant threatening to hire an attorney immediately after an accident and having a history of similar claims. Which one of the following data mining techniques would the analyst be likely to use?

a. Classification
b. Regression analysis
c. Association rule learning
d. Cluster analysis

Feedback: a. Classification is likely to be used because the insurer is predicting the category into which a member of a dataset belongs—namely the category that indicates the likely existence of fraud. The insurer intends to use characteristics known beforehand: threatening to hire an attorney immediately after the accident and having a history of similar claims with the insurer.

Association rule learning and cluster analysis are exploratory techniques and do not rely on categorizing members of a dataset based on known data characteristics. Regression analysis is used to predict a numerical value based on known data characteristics rather than a category.

Developing a Predictive Model

A data mining technique is applied to a set of data. The result of this is a model that can be applied to new data. In the example about determining whether a claim might be fraudulent, a classification technique can be used to categorize each claim. After the results are evaluated and validated, the model is used on new claims data to indicate if the claim needs to be sent for further analysis. As the model is applied over time, machine learning refines the model by analyzing the newly added data to revise the algorithms to better predict results. See the exhibit "Data Mining Used to Develop a Model."

The Data Mining Process

In 1999, a consortium of individuals who worked in the emerging field of data mining at DaimlerChrysler, NCR, and SPSS received funding from the European Union to develop a data mining process standard. The result was the **Cross Industry Standard Process for Data Mining (CRISP-DM).**[1] See the exhibit "The Cross Industry Standard Process for Data Mining (CRISP-DM)."

Cross Industry Standard Process for Data Mining (CRISP-DM)
An accepted standard for the steps in any data mining process used to provide business solutions.

A fundamental feature of this standard is the circle that surrounds the process diagram. This circle indicates that data mining is a continuous process that involves continually evaluating and refining the model.

The first step in the process is to understand what a business wants to achieve by applying data mining to one or more sets of data. For example, does an

Data Mining Used to Develop a Model

Step One

Historical Data		
Threatening to Hire Attorney	Prior Claims	Fraudulent
Y	Y	Y
N	N	N

Step Two

Data Mining Applied to Historical Data

Step Three

Develop a Predictive Model

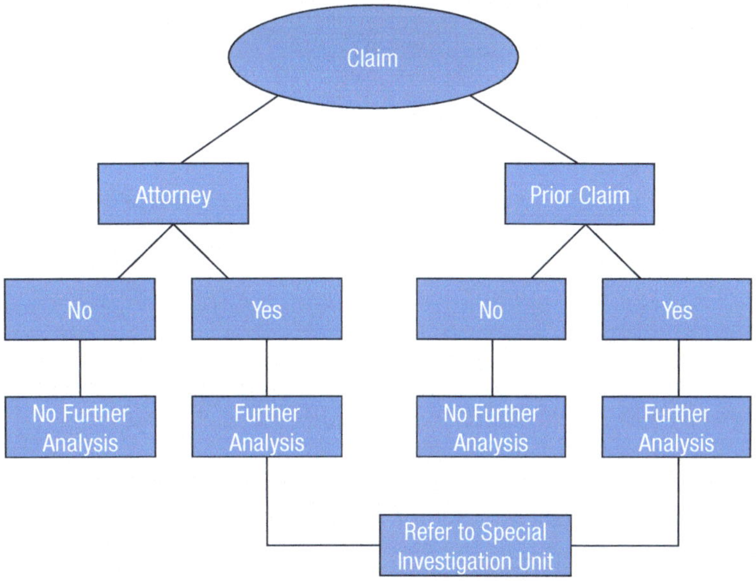

Step Four

Deploy the Model

Identify claims for further analysis

[DA11963]

The Cross Industry Standard Process for Data Mining (CRISP-DM)

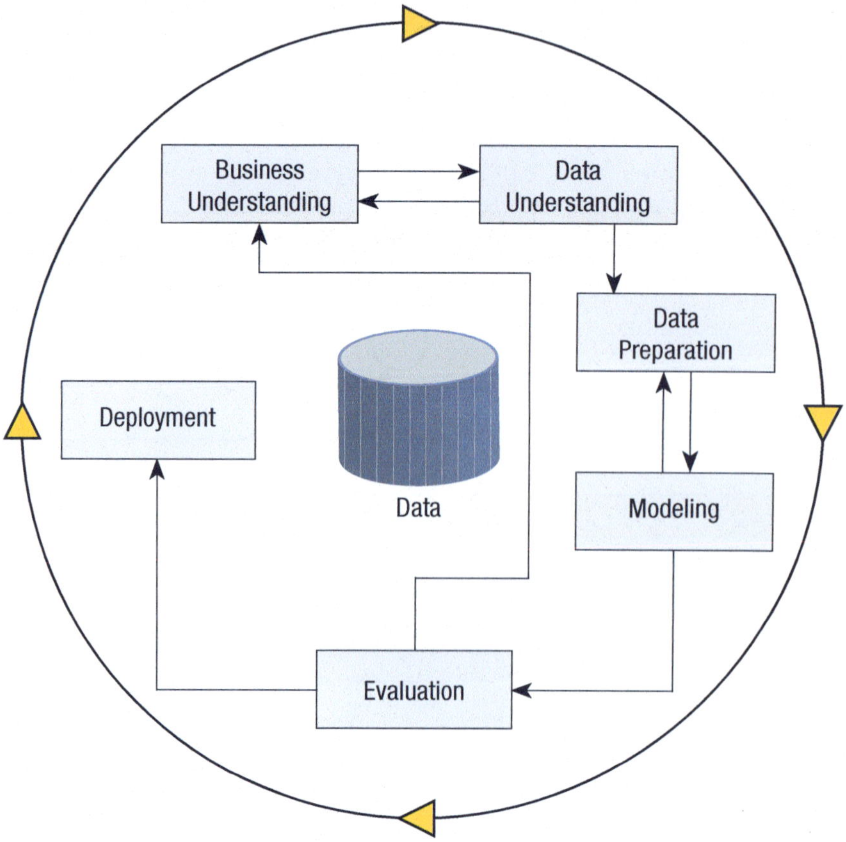

Pete Chapman (NCR), Julian Clinton (SPSS), Randy Kerber (NCR), Thomas Khabaza (SPSS), Thomas Reinartz (DaimlerChrysler), Colin Shearer (SPSS), and Rüdiger Wirth (DaimlerChrysler), CRISP-DM 1.0, SPSS, Inc., 2000, p. 10, https://the-modeling-agency.com/crisp-dm.pdf (accessed February 22, 2016). [DA11959]

insurer wish to retain more customers or better identify fraudulent claims? Does a risk manager want to find out if a wearable sensor can reduce injuries?

The next step is to understand the types of data that are being used. Is the insurer using only its own claims data, or is it also using data from a statistical rating agency? Is the risk manager only using data from sensors and its own claims data, or is the organization partnering with an insurer to obtain and analyze data?

After the data is selected and its source(s) understood, it must be prepared. This involves cleaning the data as much as possible to eliminate missing or inaccurate data. The purpose of the data mining determines to what extent the data must be cleaned. For example, if it is being used to price insurance, the data should be of high quality. However, if an insurer is exploring social media data to look for opportunities for new products, the data may be usable even if it is of lower quality.

After these steps, data mining techniques are applied to develop a model to analyze the data. The results are evaluated to determine whether they are reasonable and meet the business purpose. Even if they do not meet this purpose, the data mining may still be of use. The data might be better prepared or the model adjusted to produce the desired result. Even if the model produces useful information, machine learning will continue to refine that model to produce increasingly better and more accurate information after the model is deployed to analyze new data.

DATA SCIENCE

Big data and new technology create opportunities for data analytics to provide business solutions. However, a combination of unique skills is required to pursue these opportunities.

For insurers to gain a competitive advantage from data analytics, they must have resources with the necessary skills to gather, manage, and understand rapidly evolving types, sources, and amounts of data. Because the insurance business relies on data, insurers have typically employed individuals with the education and skills to evaluate data to determine important results, such as prices for products and claim reserves. However, without additional training in data science, these people may not have the unique skills necessary to effectively apply data analytics to newer forms of data.

Data Science Concepts

Data science is a new field at the frontier of data analytics. It uses the scientific method, which consists of these steps:

- A question or problem is raised.
- Research is conducted regarding the subject.
- A hypothesis is developed, based on the research, regarding the answer to the question or the cause of/solution to the problem.
- Experiments are performed to test the hypothesis.
- Data from the experiments is analyzed.
- A conclusion is reached.
- The conclusion is communicated.

Because data science is a new field, it is often experimental, and methods evolve rapidly. The quest of data science, as with all the sciences, is to increase knowledge of the world and provide more advanced solutions to complex questions and problems. To use an analogy, new physics analyzes the results of complex experiments to provide insights into energy, relativity, and subatomic particles that could not be fully explored by traditional physics.

Data science, like new physics, is exploring and experimenting to discover and apply new knowledge in light of the advent of big data and new methods for analyzing it.

These are four fundamental concepts of data science:

- Systematic processes can be used to discover useful knowledge from data—Insurers can benefit from a framework they can use to approach problems through data analysis. This framework can form the foundation for data-analytical processes. For example, if analysis of a dataset indicates that an insurer's auto rates are too high to compete in the market, the insurer must have a process to evaluate whether that is an accurate conclusion. If it is accurate, the insurer may be able to develop solutions to gain market share.
- Information technology can be applied to big data to reveal the characteristics of groups of people or events of interest—For example, insurers can learn the characteristics of insureds who do not renew their policies. Risk managers can identify the characteristics of employees who work safely. Underwriters can determine the characteristics of building construction that make a home or business less vulnerable to fire loss.
- Analyzing data too closely can result in interesting findings that are not generally applicable—For example, a risk manager may learn that more accidents occur after an employee's lunch break. This may be interesting, but it is unlikely to lead to an actionable conclusion. An insurer may discover that drivers between the ages of thirty-five and forty are more likely to purchase red cars, but, again, this is not useful information.
- The selection of data mining approaches and evaluation of the results must be thoughtfully considered in the context in which the results will be applied—For example, if an insurer learns the characteristics of insureds who do not renew their policies, how will the insurer use that information? Can the insurer find a way to increase retention among insureds who possess these characteristics? Could the insurer target its marketing approach to potential customers who are more likely to renew? Unless one or more actions can be taken to provide better business results, pursuing a particular data mining project may not be worthwhile.

The Data Scientist

Traditional data is usually numerical or categorical. Data scientists must be able to analyze traditional data as well as new types, including text, geolocation-based data, sensor data, images, and social network data. They must also have the skills to manage increasingly large amounts of data.

Although data science is relatively new, universities are beginning to offer courses in this field. New York University (NYU) has even created the first master of science (MS) degree program. Students are required to have strong backgrounds in mathematics, computer science, and applied statistics. NYU's program focuses on the development of new methods for data science. In its introduction to the data science master's degree program, NYU states:[2]

> Our networked world is generating a deluge of data that no human, or group of humans, can process fast enough. This data deluge has the potential to transform the way business, government, science, and healthcare are carried out. But too few possess the skills needed to use automated analytical tools and cut through the noise to create knowledge from big data.
>
> A new discipline has emerged to address the need for professionals and researchers to deal with the "data tidal wave." Its object is to provide the underlying theory and methods of the data revolution. This emergent discipline is known by several names. We call it "data science," and we have created the world's first and only MS degree program devoted to it.

Actuaries have traditionally been the insurance professionals who analyze data and make predictions based on their analyses. Actuaries have strong backgrounds in mathematics and statistics, and they must pass a rigorous series of examinations in actuarial science. Using the previous analogy of data analytics and physics, actuaries would be like the traditional physicists. They focus primarily on pricing, ratemaking, and claim reserving.

Actuary
A person who uses mathematical methods to analyze insurance data for various purposes, such as to develop insurance rates or set claim reserves.

Data scientists are like the new physicists in this analogy. They are exploring previously undiscovered realms and forces, such as social networks and new technology. The knowledge they obtain may lead to new insurance products and risk management techniques, as well as the refinement of existing products. However, there is no clear division between the roles of actuary and data scientist. Many actuaries are acquiring advanced computer programming skills using new data analysis programming languages, such as R, to supplement their mathematical and statistical knowledge.

Information related to the context for data science is often referred to as domain knowledge. While data scientists may have advanced mathematics, statistics, and computer programming knowledge, they may not have knowledge about insurance or risk management. See the exhibit "Necessary Skills for a Data Scientist."

The Data Science Team

Results produced through data science are useful only if they are relevant to the business context. Insurers must be able to gain knowledge that helps them compete more effectively to obtain benefits from data science. Similarly, risk managers must be able to employ new technologies, such as wearable devices, to improve safety or obtain new insights about risk to make data science a worthwhile endeavor for their organizations.

Risk management and insurance professionals can be valuable members of data science teams. They help provide the context for the goals of data mining projects and how results can be applied to generate business solutions. For example, underwriters may inform the insurer that it is losing commercial business to competitors. The data science team may design a data mining project to try to determine the reasons. Likewise, claims professionals may

Necessary Skills for a Data Scientist

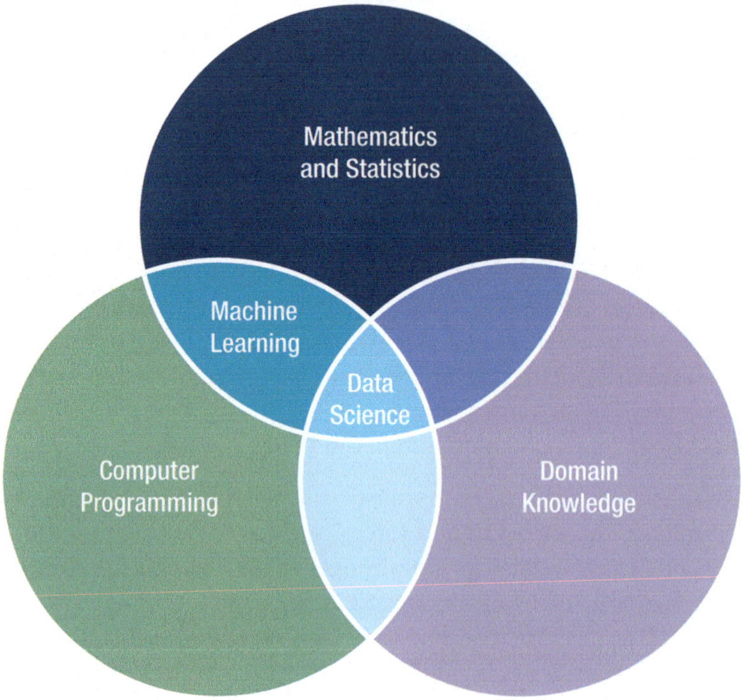

[DA12705]

find that use of opioid medications is rising, and the data science team may be able to perform data mining to analyze the characteristics of medical providers and claimants involved in excessive opioid use. Risk managers may have information regarding an increase in repetitive motion injuries; data mining may provide more detailed information on how and where those injuries are occurring, and that information may lead to a solution, such as wearable safety devices.

Apply Your Knowledge

An insurer's loss ratio is increasing. The insurer has learned through traditional data analysis that an increase in claims litigation and settlement costs seems to be the major reason. The insurer wants to determine why litigation is growing and develop potential solutions. This project will involve text mining of adjusters' notes in addition to information about jurisdiction, defense attorneys, and types of injuries. Which member of the data science team is most likely to provide domain knowledge for a project to help solve this problem?

a. Actuary

b. Data scientist

c. Claims professional

d. Underwriting professional

Feedback: c. A claims professional is the most likely team member to provide the context for this project. He or she will be familiar with litigated claims and can provide some preliminary background about factors involved. An actuary is less likely to know details about claims litigation. Similarly, an underwriter is unlikely to have detailed knowledge about this, and a data scientist would probably not have domain knowledge in this area.

DATA-DRIVEN DECISION MAKING

Risk managers and insurers have traditionally made many decisions based on data. Insurers use their own and industry loss data to price insurance products. Risk managers use accident data to reduce losses. However, data analytics can improve the types of data, methods of analysis, and results by applying **data-driven decision making**.

Data-driven decision making
An organizational process to gather and analyze relevant and verifiable data and then evaluate the results to guide business strategies.

Risk management and insurance were previously dependent on human analysis of data. Computers increasingly were able to provide data, such as losses and premiums, that could be segmented based on the business need. For example, if a risk manager or underwriter wanted to know the previous year's losses at a particular location, a computer could provide the data. The risk manager or underwriter would then analyze the data to arrive at a business decision, such as whether to renew a policy. Data science provides more advanced methods of aggregating and analyzing data.

Data Science and Data-Driven Decision Making

Data science can help insurers and risk managers improve their business results through data-driven decision making. These are several ways to achieve improvements:

- Automating decision making for improved accuracy and efficiency—For example, many insurers provide online quotes for personal auto insurance based on a computer algorithm.
- Organizing large volumes of new data—For example, an insurer could organize data according to multiple characteristics, such as the information provided by telematics, which can include speed, braking patterns, left turns, and distance traveled.
- Discovering new relationships in data—For example, a risk manager could identify the characteristics of workers who have never had a workplace

accident and use that information to identify how to improve safety for all workers.

- Exploring new sources of data—An insurer could use text mining to analyze claims adjusters' notes for various purposes, such as developing an automated system to predict a claim's severity and assign the appropriate resources to those claims predicted to become severe.

Across all types of businesses, perceived improvement in companies using big data has increased by 26 percent and is expected to increase by 41 percent in the next few years.[3] Currently, insurers process only approximately 10 to 15 percent of the available structured data.[4]

The data about using big data and data science for decision making is compelling. Insurers and risk managers have access to a wealth of existing data they are not tapping. Additionally, there is a rapidly growing quantity of external data from various sources, such as the Internet at large and the Internet of Things.

Insurers, as well as other organizations, acquire data engineering and processing technology that can manage big data, which is too large for most conventional systems. Models can then be developed to gather and analyze data in the context of an insurer's areas of interest, with results ultimately provided to the data analytics team or the manager who requested the data analysis. The appropriate person(s) can make data-driven decisions accordingly. See the exhibit "An Example of a Data-Driven Decision-Making Process."

An Example of a Data-Driven Decision-Making Process

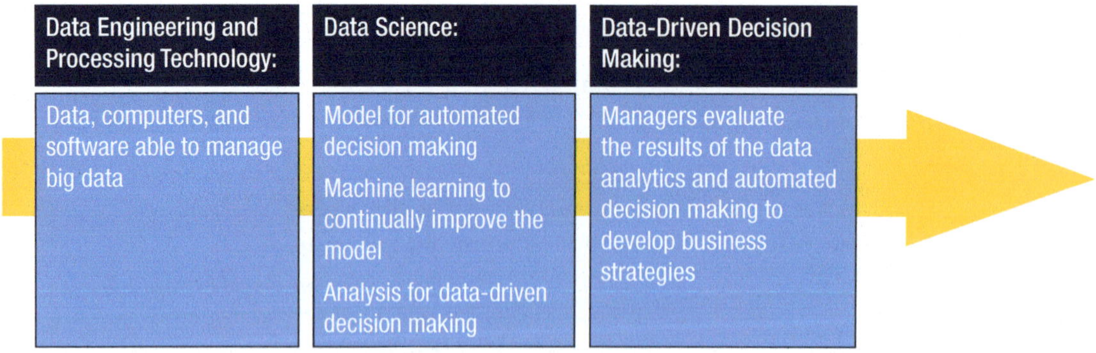

[DA11977]

Data-driven decision making can be applied across an insurer's or risk manager's enterprise to solve a variety of business problems, achieve greater efficiency, and provide a competitive advantage. There are two basic approaches to data-driven decision making: descriptive and predictive.

The Descriptive Approach

The descriptive approach is applied when an insurer or risk manager has a specific problem. Data science is intended to be used to provide data that will help solve the problem. Insurers or risk managers do not continue to use data-driven decision making beyond the specific problem.

For example, to increase market share, an insurer changed its underwriting guidelines for auto insurance one year ago. It reduced applicants' required time period without an accident to be accepted for coverage from five years to three years.

The insurer now wants to obtain data regarding the accident rates for insureds who were accepted for coverage during the past year and who qualified based on three years without an accident. The insurer also wants to compare those insureds with those accepted for coverage during the past year based on five years without an accident. Additionally, the insurer wants to compare these new customers with its previous customers. It wants data regarding previous customers' accident experience both prior to and after becoming insured.

The insurer intends to use the results of this analysis to determine if its new three-year guideline is producing acceptable results. Using data-driven decision making, executives will decide whether to continue the three-year guideline or return to the five-year guideline. This is a one-time problem for data-driven decision making, and the analysis will not be repeated.

The Predictive Approach

A predictive approach to data analytics involves providing a method that can be used repeatedly to provide information for data-driven decision making by humans, computers, or both.

For example, automated underwriting for personal auto insurance is a predictive approach that is used each time a person applies for insurance. The computer makes the underwriting decision and issues a price quote.

In another example, a risk manager may receive data from sensors regarding which employees are using required safety equipment. The risk manager will make a decision about how to address the problem of employees who are not using their safety equipment.

In an additional example, predictive analytics can be used to assign claims to an adjuster. However, the claims manager may have authority to reassign a claim that the computer assigns as a minor claim if the claim turns out to be severe.

A Model for Data-Driven Decision Making in Risk Management and Insurance

Following the process outlined in the decision-making model will help ensure the best results. The important first step is to define the risk management or insurance problem. Without a business context, modeling and analyzing data is unlikely to be effective. For example, a risk manager for a large national retailer observes that customer slips and falls are increasing in both frequency and severity. The risk manager wants to determine why this increase is occurring and develop a solution for the problem. This involves a descriptive approach because the problem requires a one-time analysis. The analytical method used for this problem will not be repeated. See the exhibit "Risk Management and Insurance Data Analytics Decision-Making Model."

Risk Management and Insurance Data Analytics Decision-Making Model

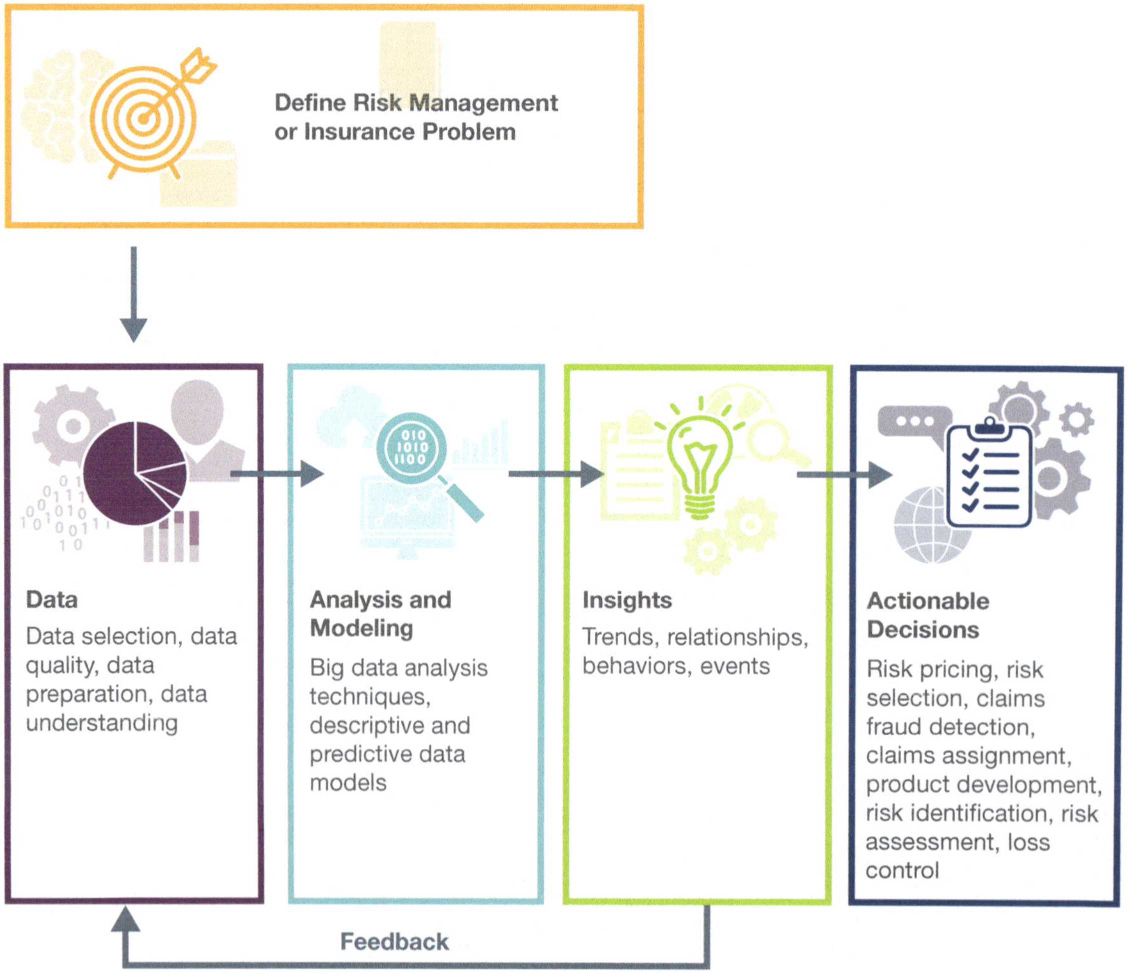

[DA11978]

The risk manager decides to focus first on the increase in frequency. The problem is clearly defined, which is the most important step in data-driven decision making. It is often useful to have input from professionals working in the area of the business where the problem is occurring. If the problem is not clearly defined, it may not be possible to make a data-driven decision.

After defining the problem, quality data must be gathered to obtain information about the customer accidents. The risk manager, who has access to the liability insurer's claims system, decides to use the insurer's claims data. The variables to be used are date of accident; store location; area of store property in which the accident occurred, such as a parking lot or entrance; weather data; and sales volume at the store on the date of accident. The risk manager runs a report to identify missing or obviously inaccurate data, such as a date of loss stated as January 1, 1898. The risk manager eliminates claims with missing or inaccurate data from the dataset.

The risk manager then meets with the data analytics team to discuss a process that will find any correlations or patterns that might be useful in analyzing the losses and the reason for the increase. Using a cluster technique, the analytics team discovers several patterns in the data: There was a spike in falls at the retailer's stores in northeastern locations in December during snowstorms. Sales volume was higher because of the holiday shopping season. Also, there was an increase in falls at the retailer's stores in Florida in August during tropical storms. Sales volume was also higher in August because of back-to-school shopping.

The risk manager is able to make several decisions driven by this data. The first decision is to provide more waterproof mats for all stores in the Northeast and Florida. Additionally, caution signs are sent to each store to be posted at the entrance during inclement weather. The risk manager reviews parking lot snow and ice removal procedures with store managers and whether salt supplies are adequate. There are also discussions with store managers in Florida about checking parking lot areas for water accumulation during storms and closing off those areas.

This example illustrates how the model for data-driven decision making can be applied in risk management and insurance contexts. The model began with the important first step of clearly defining the problem. Appropriate data was selected and prepared by removing claims with missing or inaccurate data. Relevant variables were selected. There was interaction between the risk manager and the data analytics team to discuss the problem. The data analytics team developed a method to discover patterns and correlations in the data. The risk manager was able to use the results to make a data-driven solution.

Apply Your Knowledge

A claims manager wants to learn which defense attorneys are providing the most effective outcomes. The manager selects these variables: attorney assigned to a claim, litigation expenses, length of time from attorney assignment to claim resolution, whether the claim went to trial or was settled prior to trial, amount of award or settlement, and whether an appeal was filed. Some of the data is missing the date of assignment to defense counsel and whether the claim went to trial.

Which one of the following is the first step the claims manager should take?

a. Analyze the data
b. Improve data quality
c. Select the analytical technique
d. Make a data-driven decision

Feedback: b. The first step the claims manager should take is to improve the data quality, as the manager has already defined the problem—finding which defense attorneys are providing the most effective outcomes. There are problems with data quality, because two data fields are missing some of the claims. Therefore, the claims manager will need to have those fields completed or eliminate the claims with missing fields from the dataset. The data analytics team will select the analytical technique. It is not possible to make a data-driven decision at this stage of the process.

SUMMARY

Although insurance has always involved data analytics, technology and big data provide many more sources and a much larger quantity of data. The additional sources and quantity of data now available cannot be organized and analyzed with traditional techniques. Data science is a new field that provides methods to obtain data from new sources such as the Internet and the Internet of Things. It also provides methods to organize and analyze the data to provide relevant knowledge. Organizations can then use that knowledge strategically to improve business decisions.

Big data has various characteristics and sources that distinguish it from traditional data. The characteristics include not only the amount of data, but also its accuracy, whether it is structured or unstructured, its velocity, and the value it adds to an insurer's business decisions. Sources include an insurer's own internal data and external data, both structured and unstructured. By applying data science techniques to big data, insurers can increase their access to useful information to guide their business decisions and strategies.

Accurate, appropriate, reasonable, and comprehensive data is necessary to perform useful analysis. Data quality has always been a concern for insurers, but with increases in the volume and variety of data, these concerns have also increased. One way insurers address these concerns is through the use of metadata. In addition, analysts employ various methods to detect incorrect or missing data. Data security is also an important consideration in ensuring quality data; it can help maintain the quality of an insurer's data.

Data mining is the application of techniques, such as classification, regression analysis, association rule learning, and cluster analysis, to develop models that can be used to analyze big data. CRISP-DM is a standard process for data mining that organizations should use to obtain business solutions from big data.

Data science has recently emerged as a new scientific field in response to the convergence of big data and technology. Because traditional skills and methods are insufficient to handle the rapid changes in the amounts and types of data, professionals with a unique combination of knowledge and skills are necessary to explore this new information frontier and provide useful business solutions. Because domain knowledge is an important aspect of data science, insurance and risk management professionals are often important members of data science teams to provide a business context.

Although risk managers and insurers have traditionally made decisions based on data, the amount and sources of data have increased exponentially and will continue to do so. Additionally, the methods to gather, process, and analyze data have also increased and become more sophisticated. To gain competitive advantage and operate more effectively, insurers and risk managers must be able to frame business problems and questions and use the techniques of data science to perform analysis that will improve results.

ASSIGNMENT NOTES

1. Foster Provost and Tom Fawcett, "Data Science for Business" (Sebastopol, Calif.: O'Reilly Media, Inc., 2013), p. 26.
2. "Educating the Next Generation of Data Scientists," New York University, http://cds.nyu.edu/academics/ms-in-data-science/ (accessed March 9, 2016).
3. Economist Intelligence Unit, "The Deciding Factor: Big Data and Decision Making," Business Analytics, www.uk.capgemini.com/resource-file-access/resource/pdf/The_Deciding_Factor__Big_Data___Decision_Making.pdf (accessed March 15, 2016).
4. Ajay Bhargava, "A Dozen Ways Insurers Can Leverage Big Data for Business Value," Tata Consultancy Services White Paper, www.tcs.com/resources/white_papers/Pages/Business-Value-Big-Data-Insurers.aspx (accessed March 15, 2016).

Direct Your Learning

2

Predictive Modeling Concepts

Educational Objectives

After learning the content of this assignment, you should be able to:

- Describe these modeling concepts:
  - Supervised versus unsupervised learning
  - Predictive versus descriptive modeling
  - Algorithms
  - Entropy
  - Lift
- Explain how similarity and distance are used in data modeling.
- Explain how to train and evaluate a predictive model.

Outline

Predictive Modeling Concepts

2

BASIC MODELING CONCEPTS

Insurers increasingly rely on data mining to help them make more informed underwriting, claims, and marketing decisions. Data modeling is the key to transforming raw data into something more useful. Understanding the basic modeling terms and types of models can help insurance and risk management professionals effectively communicate with data scientists to create models that will benefit the insurance industry.

In the data mining process, modeling is the representation of data; this representation is then used to define and analyze the data. Modeling data is a complex process that uses concepts from both machine learning and statistics. Actuaries and data scientists select the appropriate methods for modeling based on the type of data available and their particular goal in analyzing it. These are some common modeling concepts:

- Supervised versus unsupervised learning
- Predictive versus descriptive modeling
- Algorithms
- Entropy
- Lift

Supervised Versus Unsupervised Learning

There are two main types of data mining techniques: supervised and unsupervised. Both are used to find patterns in large datasets. The terms "supervised learning" and "unsupervised learning" come from the field of machine learning.

If the goal of the data mining (the target) is known—for example, if an insurance company wants to know whether auto policyholders under the age of thirty are more likely to have an accident than those over thirty—the process is called **supervised learning**.

Supervised learning
A type of model creation, derived from the field of machine learning, in which the target variable is defined.

An **unsupervised learning** method of data mining is conducted when there is no defined target. For example, the same insurance company might simply ask whether auto policyholders fall into natural groupings. There is no intended answer to this query, and the company will look at the results to find any meaningful groups or patterns. While this can be beneficial, a danger of unsupervised learning is that it can easily reveal meaningless correlations—

Unsupervised learning
A type of model creation, derived from the field of machine learning, that does not have a defined target variable.

for example, that policyholders named John are more likely to have auto accidents.

However, a challenge of supervised learning is that there must be data about the target. To return to the previous example, if no data exists about drivers under thirty, there is nothing to study. Conducting unsupervised learning first may provide the information needed to define an appropriate target for supervised learning.

Predictive Versus Descriptive Modeling

The concepts of predictive and descriptive modeling reflect those of supervised and unsupervised learning in that the main difference between predictive and descriptive modeling lies in what is defined. A **predictive model** is used to estimate a target value. Although the value itself is unknown, the intent of the model is clear. For example, if an auto insurer wants to know how many of its third-party bodily injury claims will exceed $25,000, it might use a predictive model. Predictive models are not limited to predicting the future; they can be used to determine unknown values in the past or present.

Predictive model
A model used to predict an unknown outcome by means of a defined target variable.

A **descriptive model**, by comparison, is used to study data and gain insight into it. For example, an auto insurer might want to know what third-party bodily injury claimants with large claims are like and what similarities they have. The information gained from descriptive models can be used to build predictive models. To continue the example, if a disproportionate number of third-party bodily injury claimants live in the state of Texas, an actuary or a data scientist could use the attribute of how many policyholders live in Texas to gain insight into the insurer's number of large third-party bodily injury claims.

Descriptive model
A model used to study and find relationships within data.

A sample of the data used to develop a predictive model can help define the terms that actuaries and data scientists use, such as **attribute**, **instance (example)**, and **target variable**. Assume that the data in the exhibit is being used to develop a model that predicts the likelihood that homeowners insurance policyholders will not renew their policies. Because the sample instances are being used to develop a predictive model, they include known values of the target variable as well as the values of each attribute. See the exhibit "Predictive Modeling Data Example: Homeowners Insurance."

Attribute
A variable that describes a characteristic of an instance within a model.

Instance (example)
The representation of a data point described by a set of attributes within a model's dataset.

Target variable
The predefined attribute whose value is being predicted in a data analytical model.

In the sample, the target variable is a binary variable, meaning that it can have only one of two answers—yes or no. The **class label** is the value of the target variable (in this case, yes or no).

Class label
The value of the target variable in a model.

Algorithms

Modeling software—both descriptive and predictive—uses algorithms to mine data and to analyze it. After an insurer selects the business objectives of its model and the data that will be analyzed, an algorithm is selected. An algorithm is a set of steps used to solve a problem or complete a process.

Predictive Modeling Data Example: Homeowners Insurance

	Attribute	Attribute	Attribute	Attribute	Target variable
	Name	Age	Length of Time With Insurer	Premium	Policy Not Renewed
Instance	Anna	33	3 years	$750	Yes
Instance	Carlos	45	7 years	$825	No
Instance	David	50	15 years	$600	No
Instance	Jason	27	4 years	$725	Yes
Instance	Sonia	28	2 years	$550	No

[DA11964]

Strictly speaking, an algorithm is different from a model, which is an attempt to represent the state of something. In the world of data analytics, though, the terms "algorithm" and "model" are often used interchangeably. Machine learning algorithms can take a number of forms, such as mathematical equations, classification trees, and clustering techniques. Experienced actuaries and data scientists have the expertise needed to select which algorithm is appropriate for a particular problem.

Entropy

An issue that arises in modeling is the question of which attribute being examined has the greatest value to the data scientist. An attribute's value is measured in terms of **information gain** and **entropy**. Entropy is essentially a measure of how unpredictable something is, while information gain can be thought of in terms of how much it affects the entropy of a given dataset, which is also an indication of how much information it provides about the target variable.

Information gain
A measure of the predictive power of one or more attributes.

Entropy
A measure of disorder in a dataset.

For example, if an insurer is trying to determine which homeowners insurance customers are most likely to not renew their policies based on the policyholders' age, length of time with the insurer, and policy premium, it will need to determine which attributes correlate most closely with the decision to not renew. If customers who have been with the insurer longer than five years are likely to renew their policies, that attribute—length of time with the insurer—is useful; it has high information gain, which means that it decreases entropy.

The example is a visual representation of the entropy of the described dataset. Each *Y* and *N* represents a class label of "yes, will not renew," or "no, will not renew (will renew)." When the dataset is segmented based on informative attributes (those with high information gain), the entropy decreases. See the exhibit "Entropy Example."

Entropy Example

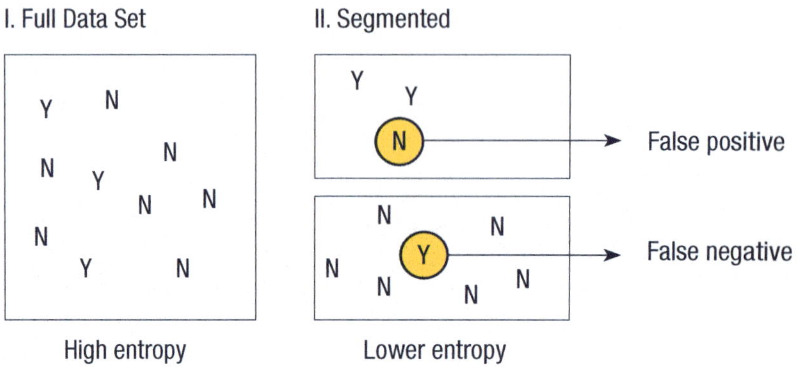

In II, the dataset is segmented based on attributes that provide information gain as to whether the policyholder will decide not to renew a homeowners policy. The predictive model used to label the instances in II produces one false positive and one false negative result.

[DA11965]

Lift

Lift
In model performance evaluation, the percentage of positive predictions made by the model divided by the percentage of positive predictions that would be made in the absence of the model.

One way of understanding the value a model brings to a business is through the concept of **lift**. It is particularly useful in a marketing context, as it can evaluate the effectiveness of targeting customers according to the results of a model versus randomly marketing to customers.

In the context of modeling, the word "positive" means that the model is predicting that the item of interest will occur, even if it is commonly considered to be a negative outcome. For example, a model that predicts fraud has occurred is said to produce a positive result.

Returning to the example of predicting homeowners insurance applicants' likelihood of not renewing their policies, assume that an insurer wants to test the effectiveness of the predictive model. The insurer has data on 1,000 customers, 300 of whom did not renew. As a test, the insurer uses the model to rank these according to the likelihood that each would not renew, which it calculates using the customers' attributes. The insurer finds that the model would have identified 50 percent of the customers who did not renew (150) if it had been applied to only 20 percent (200) of the customers it identified in rank order. Without the model—that is, by chance—on average, only 20 percent (60) of the customers who did not renew would have been identified. The lift is calculated in this way: 0.50 ÷ 0.20 = 2.5. See the exhibit "Lift Curve Example: Homeowners Insurance."

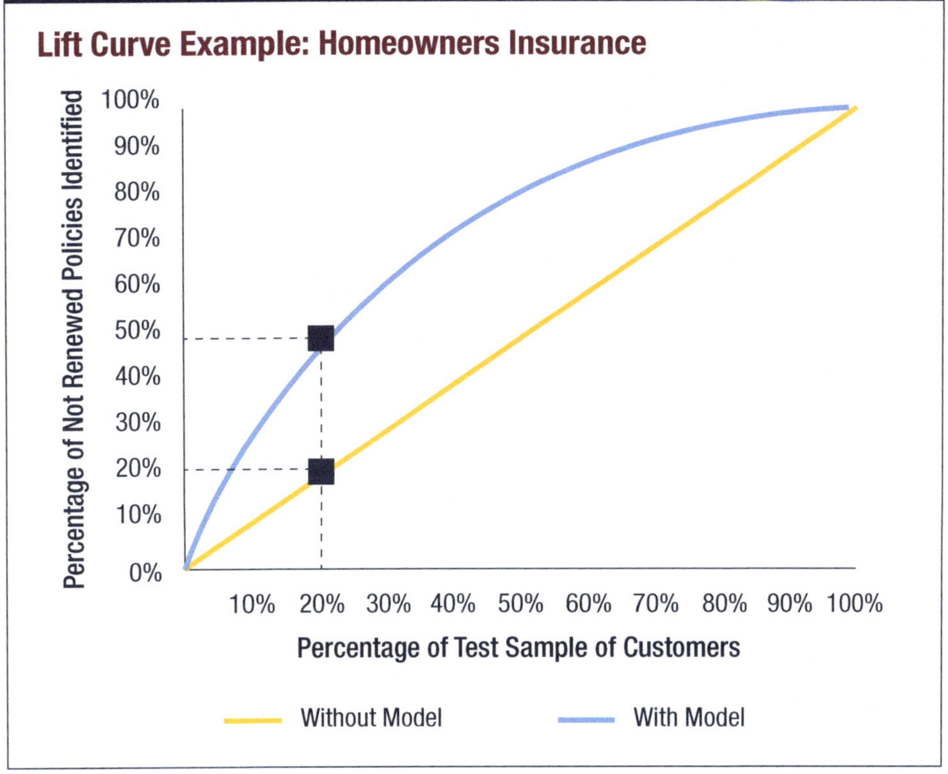

[DA11966]

Leverage, an alternative measure of a model's accuracy, examines the difference between the two outcomes. For this example, leverage would be calculated in this way: 0.50 – 0.20 = 0.30.

Measuring lift and leverage is an effective way for insurance and risk management professionals to evaluate predictive models and know how reliable they are. For example, a claims department may need to know the ability of a predictive model to prioritize potentially fraudulent claims.

Leverage
In model performance evaluation, the percentage of positive predictions made by the model minus the percentage of positive predictions that would be made in the absence of the model.

Apply Your Knowledge

You are a property claims representative, and your claims manager has asked you to work with a data scientist to determine why claims have increased over the past six months. The increase has been across several different regions, and your claims manager is not sure whether there is a common factor in the claims. Based on the information you currently have, which one of these is most appropriate?

a. A predictive model
b. A descriptive model
c. A target variable
d. A lift curve

Feedback: b. At this point, with no specific target, a descriptive model would be most appropriate for studying the data surrounding the claims and looking for any patterns in it. If there is a high number of property damage claims among, for example, policyholders filing for divorce, you could use a predictive model with recent divorce filings as an attribute and the number of property claims as the target variable. A lift curve could be used to show whether the predictive model is effective.

SIMILARITY AND DISTANCE

By now, most people are accustomed to receiving tailored marketing messages that are based on their similarities to other consumers. Movie recommendations, grocery store coupons, and online travel ads are all based on data that shows how similar one consumer is to another. This concept is being expanded into the insurance and risk management industry so that not only purchasing habits but also claims frequency, financial stability, and insurer loyalty can be predicted.

Unsupervised data mining searches for similarities, which can then become the basis of predictive data modeling. The distances between instances (examples), identified through data points, can be measured to find instances that are most similar. Finding similar data is valuable to businesses, because through the concepts of nearest neighbors and link prediction, behaviors and information flow can be predicted.

Measuring Similarity and Distance

Similarity is the measure of how alike two data objects are. The objective of most data modeling is to find the similarity between data points (instances). Determining which similarities are significant can be subjective, however. For example, if an auto insurer was studying a group of policyholders to find similarities, would it want to place much weight on policyholders' having the same name? Would that name make their driving habits and insurance purchases similar? Probably not. Other similarities would be more meaningful, such as the home cities and ages of the policyholders and the conditions of policyholders' vehicles.

Despite the limitation of subjectivity, meaningful similarities are extremely useful to businesses. If an insurer can find similar claims, it may be able to predict settlement amounts, defense costs, and the likelihood of fraud.

Once a data scientist has determined the value of the attributes that make up an instance, a data point that represents the value of the instance's target variable is plotted on a graph. In a data mining context, similarity is usually measured as the distance between two instances' data points. A small distance indicates a high degree of similarity, and a large distance indicates a low degree of similarity.

For the distance between two points to accurately depict their similarity, adjustments sometimes are made to ensure that all attributes influencing distance do so proportionally, as opposed to one attribute influencing distance more than it should. For example, if a personal auto insurer is comparing two policyholders by the number of miles they drive each year and by the number of years they have been with the insurer and accident free, the number of miles will be a higher number. It will therefore have a greater effect on the distance although it is not necessarily a more important attribute. A data scientist would scale the variable of miles driven to make the measure of similarity more accurate.

Measuring the distance between two data points can indicate their inherent similarity. For example, suppose a commercial lines insurer wants to evaluate the underwriting risk of insuring Company B. The insurer knows some information about Company B, but not enough to know for sure whether it's an acceptable risk. But what if it could compare Company B with Company A, a business with which the insurer has worked for years and that represents an acceptable risk?

The insurer could work with a data scientist to decide which of Company A's attributes indicate a good risk. In the exhibit, two of Company A's attributes are represented numerically, and a data point that accounts for the attributes is plotted on the graph. A numerical representation of those same attributes is also plotted for Company B. By creating a triangle, the distance—and therefore similarity—between the two companies can be measured. See the exhibit "Using Distance to Measure Similarity."

Applications of Similarity and Distance

Businesses, including insurers, can apply the concept of similarity and distance to help them understand their customers and predict behavior. These predictions can be valuable planning resources.

Nearest Neighbors

Measuring the distance between instances determines which instances are **nearest neighbors**.

Nearest neighbor
The most similar instance in a data model.

Suppose a property-casualty insurer has had an increase in fraudulently padded claims. To save claims representatives time and to best use the special investigation unit (SIU), the insurer wishes to refer claims that are most likely fraudulent to the SIU directly.

Working with a data scientist, the insurer could, as a first step, compile a list of general claims attributes. For example, an attribute of a claim could be the claimant's age. Another attribute could be the number of days it took the

Using Distance to Measure Similarity

One attribute is represented on the *X* axis, and the other attribute is represented on the *Y* axis. The vertical distance between the two points is the difference between Y_B and Y_A. The horizontal distance is the difference between X_B and X_A. These two distance measures form the sides of a right triangle. The distance between *A* and *B* can then be measured by calculating the hypotenuse of the triangle.

This is a simplified example. If more than two attributes are being compared, which is often the case, the data points are plotted in a space with more than two dimensions. For example, three attributes would be plotted in a three-dimensional space.

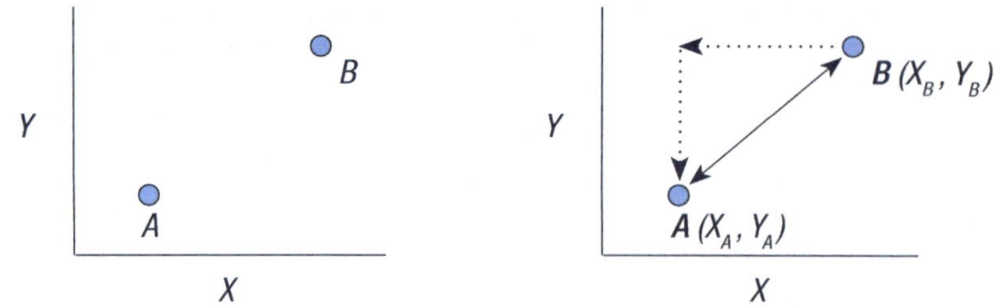

[DA11960]

claimant to report the claim. Each claim can be represented as a data point, plotted, and measured by the distance between each other claim. The insurer may find that many fraudulent claims are plotted near each other and may therefore be able to predict padded claims based on new claims' similarity to known padded claims.

Continuing with the property-casualty insurer example, assume that the insurer receives a new claim and that the related instance has three nearest neighbors with known values for the target variables: two fraudulent claims and one nonfraudulent claim. The algorithms for nearest neighbors often use the shorthand **k nearest neighbor (k-NN)**, with the "k" referring to the number of neighbors used—which, in this example, would be 3-NN.

k nearest neighbor (k-NN)
An algorithm in which "k" equals the number of nearest neighbors plotted on a graph.

Combining function
The combination of two functions to form a new function.

Using a majority **combining function**, the majority of the nearest neighbors' values predict the class label of the target variable. In this case, yes, a fraudulent claim can be confirmed.

The exhibit shows the placement of the nearest neighbors described in the example. See the exhibit "Nearest Neighbor Example: Fraudulent Claims."

Using the majority combining function gives equal weight to all of the nearest neighbors. It does not consider their distance, and the three claims are not an equal distance from the claim in question.

Assume that Claim A has a distance of twelve, Claim B has a distance of thirteen, and Claim C has a distance of twenty. Their contributions to the average can be weighted by their distance.

Nearest Neighbor Example: Fraudulent Claims

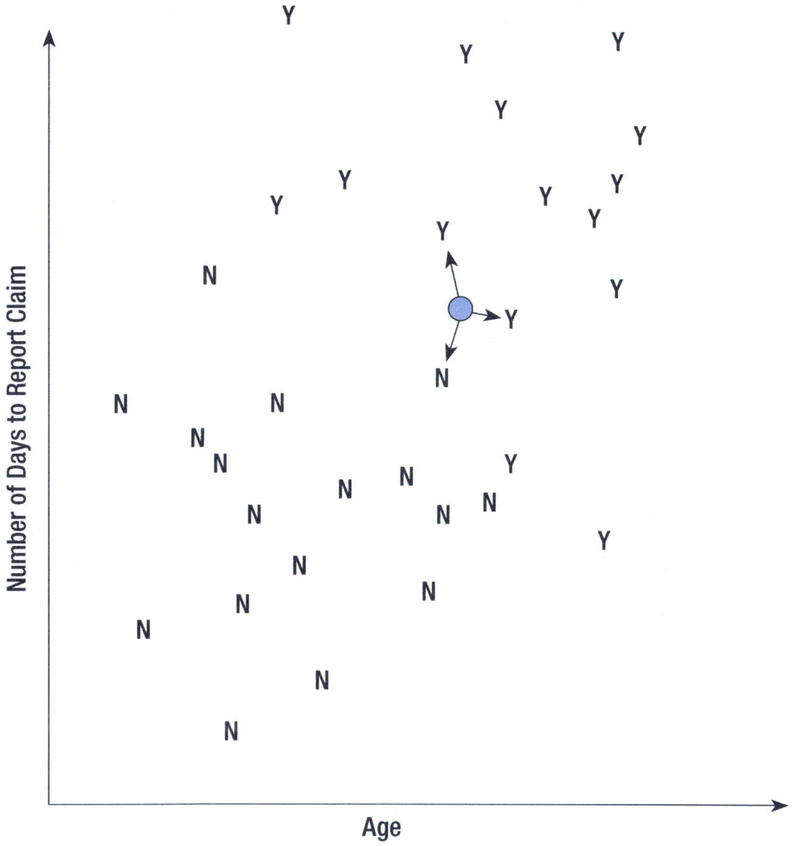

[DA11961]

Claims A and B should contribute relatively more to the weighting because they are closer to the claim in question than Claim C. To calculate the contributions, each distance amount is squared, and the reciprocal of the square is calculated, resulting in a similarity weight. The similarity weights are then weighted relative to each other so that they total 1.00, resulting in a contribution amount. To calculate a probability estimate for each claim, a score of 1.00 is assigned to "Yes," and a score of 0.00 is assigned to "No," with these numbers multiplied by the respective contribution amounts. See the exhibit "Weighted Average Example: Fraudulent Claims."

Weighted Average Example: Fraudulent Claims

Claim	Distance	Similarity Weight	Contribution	Class
Claim A	12	0.0069	0.4521	Yes
Claim B	13	0.0059	0.3852	No
Claim C	20	0.0025	0.1627	Yes

Based on the contribution amount and the class assignment, the probability estimates are 0.61 (0.45 + 0.16) that the claim will be fraudulent and 0.39 that it will not. This technique provides a more accurate estimate than a simple majority combining function.

This material is based on concepts from Foster Provost and Tom Fawcett, Data Science for Business (Sebastopol, Calif.: O'Reilly Media, Inc., 2013), p. 150. [DA11962]

Measuring Similarity in Networks

Similarity does not always have to be measured as the distance on a graph. It can also be examined through network connections. Insurers can examine social networks and gain information about their customers based on their similarities.

Link prediction

A prediction of the connection between data items.

In **link prediction**, a model attempts to predict a pair of instances. It does this by measuring the similarities between the two instances. In practice, this means that a model can use people's similarities to predict who will be friends with whom on Facebook or what movies a person will want to watch on Netflix.

Centrality measures can also be used to examine connections. In a social networking scenario, degree counts how many people are connected to a person—for example, how many friends a person has on Facebook. Closeness measures the distance from these people (friends) to the central person—essentially, the similarity between them—and therefore how quickly information will travel between them.

Betweenness measures the extent to which a person connects others. For example, Susan could be connected to Chris because they are both friends with Maria. Information that Susan posts on Facebook could travel to Chris through Maria. If Maria connects many people in this way, she would be considered to have a high degree of betweenness.

Information from social networks can give insurance professionals and risk managers insight into customers' purchases, health, and risky behaviors.

TRAINING AND EVALUATING A PREDICTIVE MODEL

Many organizations, including insurers, use predictive models to guide future business decisions. For example, proper implementation of predictive modeling can improve an insurer's consistency and efficiency in marketing, underwriting, and claims services by helping to define target markets, increasing the number of policy price points, and reducing claims fraud. Understandably, businesses are cautious about relying on predictive models. Therefore, during the development of predictive models, businesses must be able to assess the models' effectiveness and reliability.

One way in which insurance professionals and risk managers can employ predictive modeling to their advantage is to help them anticipate behaviors. For example, if an organization can predict which of its employees are likely to have workplace injuries, it could develop strategies to improve these employees' on-the-job safety. The organization could use the data it has about its past and current employees to create a predictive model that would use what it learned about those employees to determine the likelihood of workplace injuries among current and future employees.

Suppose that a clothing manufacturer is developing a predictive model to do just this. The first step in building the predictive model is to supply it with data about employees who did and did not have accidents. The manufacturer decides to limit the data it uses to that from the past year. The manufacturer then comes up with fifteen attributes that describe each employee, such as the shift he or she works, experience on the job, and whether he or she uses a safety device.

Now assume that the model is made to account for each of the fifteen attributes as they appear in the dataset. The model is then used on the **training data**, and the model appears to be very accurate. The manufacturer is pleased with the results of the model and decides to move it into production, where it will make real-life predictions about employees. When the model is run in the production environment, only 1 percent of the employees are flagged as likely to have an accident. The manufacturer's risk manager, who is examining the results, knows that this cannot be correct, because, according to historical data, roughly 5 percent of the manufacturer's employees have an accident every year. What went wrong? Why is the model that was so effective in the training environment no longer valid?

Training data
Data that is used to train a predictive model and that therefore must have known values for the target variable of the model.

Most likely, the model was tailored too closely to the training data. This mistake could have been avoided by initially saving some of the training data for evaluation and by applying performance metrics to the model before moving it into production. See the exhibit "The Process of Training and Evaluating a Predictive Model."

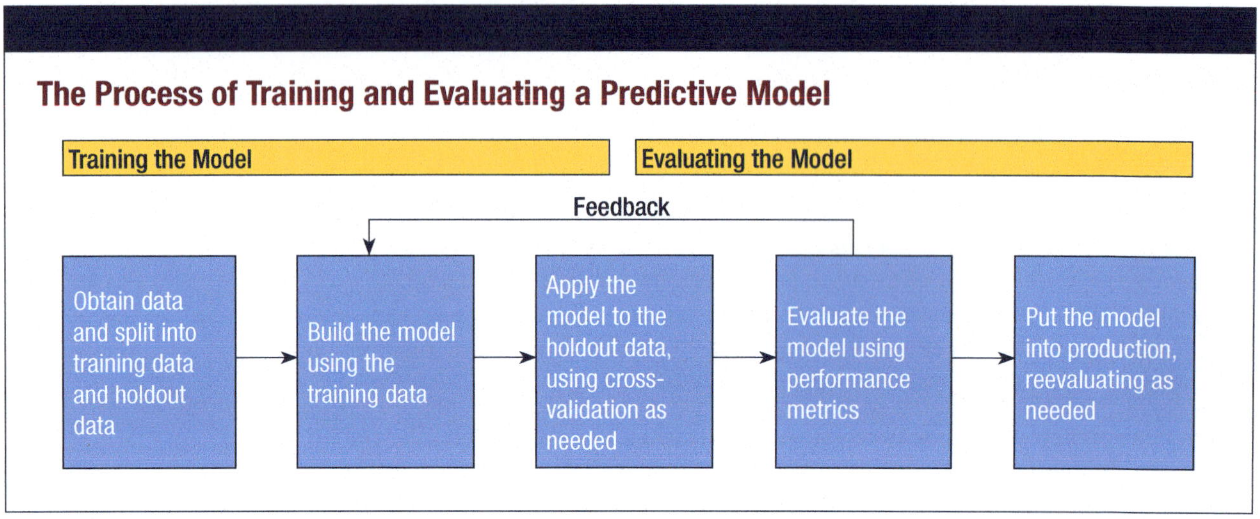

[DA11972]

Training the Model

A predictive model is trained using data that has known values for the target variable. In the example of the workplace injury predictive model, the class labels of the target variable are "yes, workplace accident," and "no, no workplace accident."

Training Data

The selection of attributes to use in a predictive model determines the model's success, and the selection must often be fine-tuned several times. For the workplace injury predictive model, the insurer selected fifteen attributes to describe each instance (example). The model must be made complex enough to be accurate. If the model used only the attributes of shift and safety device, that might not provide enough information to make accurate predictions. However, if too many attributes are used, a model can easily overfit the training data.

Overfitting
The process of fitting a model too closely to the training data for the model to be effective on other data.

Overfitting occurs when a model is overly tailored to the training data.[1] For example, suppose that in the workplace injury training data, a correlation happened to exist between second-shift employees and workplace injuries. In the model training environment, this seems significant. However, it could easily turn out to be a random peculiarity of the training data. To check whether the correlation between second-shift employees and workplace injuries is significant or an anomaly, the manufacturer can use holdout data.

Holdout data
In the model training process, existing data with a known target variable that is not used as part of the training data.

Holdout Data

Holdout data is data that is held out from the training data. Like the training data, the holdout data must have known class labels for the model's target variable. The holdout data is used to test the model to make sure it performs well on data that was not used in its development and, therefore, helps ensure that the model is not overfitted to the training data.

Using the holdout data, the predictive model indicates a correlation between second-shift employees and workplace injuries that is similar to that it discovered in the training data. This is a good indication that the model can apply **generalization**. As illustrated in the exhibit, the model must have some complexity to be accurate, but if it has too much complexity (in other words, it is overfit), it will not be accurate beyond the training data. See the exhibit "Complexity of a Model."

Generalization

The ability of a model to apply itself to data outside the training data.

Complexity of a Model

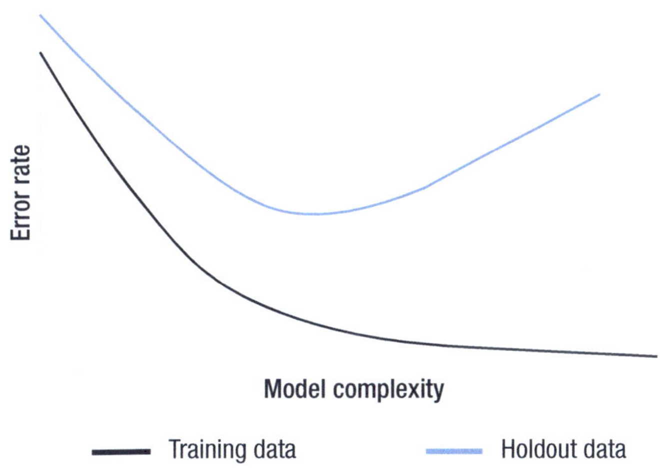

[DA11973]

Cross-Validation

Sometimes, a model's performance on the holdout data will not sufficiently reassure its developers that it will perform well in production. For example, the risk manager at the clothing manufacturer may not be comfortable flagging employees for additional safety training after seeing only the predictive model's performance on the training data and holdout data. At other times, a very limited amount of training data may be available, and the model's developers may think it unwise to not use some of the data for training because of the need for holdout data. In either one of these scenarios, cross-validation may be the appropriate solution.

Cross-validation is the process of splitting the available data into multiple folds and then using different folds of the data for model training and holdout testing. The result is that all of the data is used in both ways, and the predictive model is developed in several ways, allowing its developers to choose the version that performs best. The selected model can then be trained using the entire dataset. See the exhibit "Cross-Validation."

Cross-Validation

Total data (split into three folds)		
1	2	3
Model 1		
Holdout data	Training data	Training data
Model 2		
Training data	Holdout data	Training data
Model 3		
Training data	Training data	Holdout data

[DA11974]

Evaluating the Model

Before a business uses a predictive model, its effectiveness on data with which it was not trained should be evaluated. Evaluation also continues after the training and testing process ends, when a business moves a model to production and can see its true effectiveness with new data.

Performance Metrics

Various metrics can be used to evaluate a model's performance. This section examines evaluation methods that are particularly useful when a model is predicting a categorical class label. The performance metrics can be best understood in terms of a "confusion matrix" that presents the results of a predictive model on a dataset. See the exhibit "Confusion Matrix Example: Clothing Manufacturer Workplace Injuries."

A data scientist or an actuary can recommend the best evaluation methods for a particular model, including these:[2]

Accuracy
In model performance evaluation, a model's correct predictions divided by its total predictions.

- **Accuracy**—This is simply a measure of how often the model predicts the correct outcome:

$$(TP + TN) \div (TP + TN + FP + FN)$$

Confusion Matrix Example: Clothing Manufacturer Workplace Injuries

Assume that a predictive model is applied to the clothing manufacturer's data of 1,000 employees, 50 of whom had workplace injuries in the past year. How often did the model correctly and incorrectly predict for each employee "yes, will have an accident" or "no, will not have an accident"?

	Predicted No	+	Predicted Yes	=	Total (1,000 Employees)
Actual No	945		5		950
Actual Yes	10		40		50

Based on the preceding numbers, these statements can be made:

- There are 40 true positives (TP) for which the model correctly predicted yes.
- There are 945 true negatives (TN) for which the model correctly predicted no.
- There are 5 false positives (FP) for which the model incorrectly predicted yes (and the actual answer is no).
- There are 10 false negatives (FN) for which the model incorrectly predicted no (and the actual answer is yes).

This material is adapted from "Simple guide to confusion matrix terminology," Data School, March 26, 2014, www.dataschool.io/simple-guide-to-confusion-matrix-terminology (accessed March 18, 2016). [DA11975]

Based on the numbers in the exhibit, the accuracy of the workplace injury predictive model is calculated as (40 + 945) ÷ (40 + 945 + 5 + 10) = 0.985.

- **Precision**—Instead of looking at the total results of a model, precision measures only the positive results and is usually a better measure of a model's success than accuracy:

$$TP \div (TP + FP)$$

Based on the numbers in the exhibit, the precision of the workplace injury predictive model is calculated as 40 ÷ (40 + 5) = 0.889.

- **Recall**—This is a measure of how well the model catches positive results:

$$TP \div (TP + FN)$$

Based on the numbers in the exhibit, the recall of the workplace injury predictive model is calculated as 40 ÷ (40 + 10) = 0.80.

- **F-score**—This is a popular way of evaluating a predictive model because it takes into account both the precision and recall measures:

$$2 \times ([\text{Precision} \times \text{recall}] \div [\text{Precision} + \text{recall}])$$

Precision
In model performance evaluation, a model's correct positive predictions divided by its total positive predictions.

Recall
In model performance evaluation, a model's correct positive predictions divided by the sum of its correct positive predictions and incorrect negative predictions.

F-score
In statistics, the measure that combines precision and recall and is the harmonic mean of precision and recall.

Based on the numbers in the previous equations, the workplace injury predictive model's F-score is calculated as $2 \times [(0.889 \times 0.80) \div (0.889 + 0.80)] = 0.842$.

Putting the Model Into Production

Once a predictive model is placed in production (or used by a business in its daily operations), the training process does not end. It is only at this point that a model's true value will be proved. If a model's predictions do not guide good business decisions, then the model should be reevaluated. Returning to the workplace injury predictive model example, if one year after the model has been used in production, the manufacturer's risk manager finds that it has been flagging the wrong employees as being likely to have an accident and that the company has wasted resources providing additional safety training for these employees, the model should be retrained and reevaluated.

Insurance and risk management professionals should also defer to their professional experience when examining a model's results. If the results do not seem to make sense, there is a good chance that the model was overfitted or is not complex enough. Insurance professionals and risk managers should also keep in mind that situations change. No predictive model will make accurate predictions indefinitely. When significant economic, technological, or cultural changes occur, they should work with data scientists or actuaries to update predictive models and retrain them to provide the best results.

Apply Your Knowledge

You are an underwriter charged with working with a team of data scientists to develop a model that predicts which college-student policyholders will continue to receive good grades and therefore receive good-student discounts on their auto insurance. Your employer is hopeful that the model could eliminate the necessity of having every good-student policyholder mail his or her grade transcript to the insurer. Your manager is concerned that the data scientists are training the model with only 80 percent of the data you supplied about student drivers. What would be an appropriate response?

Feedback: An appropriate response would be an explanation of holdout data—data with a known target variable that is saved to test the model with after it has been trained. The data scientists are clearly experienced enough to know this important step of model training and evaluation.

SUMMARY

To communicate effectively with data scientists, insurance and risk management professionals should be familiar with basic modeling concepts, such as supervised and unsupervised learning, predictive and descriptive modeling, algorithms, entropy, and lift curves. The more familiar insurance professionals are with these concepts, the better they will be able to help create and interpret models based on insurance industry data.

Data scientists use the concepts of similarity, distance, nearest neighbors, and link prediction to forecast behavior and trends. Understanding these concepts can help insurance and risk management professionals use data modeling across the industry, rather than solely in a marketing context.

Training and evaluating a predictive model involves separating data into training and holdout data, training the model, evaluating the model through various performance metrics and retraining it as needed, and then moving the model into production. Insurance and risk management professionals should be aware of the limitations of models—they can be too complex or not complex enough, and they must be reevaluated frequently. Working with experienced model developers can ensure that predictive models make precise business predictions.

ASSIGNMENT NOTES

1. Foster Provost and Tom Fawcett, Data Science for Business (Sebastopol, Calif.: O'Reilly Media, Inc., 2013), p. 113.
2. Cathy O'Neill and Rachel Schutt, Doing Data Science (Sebastopol, Calif.: O'Reilly Media, 2014), pp. 127, 240–241.

Direct Your Learning

3

Traditional Analysis Techniques for Big Data

Educational Objectives

After learning the content of this assignment, you should be able to:

- Summarize traditional data analysis techniques and their application to risk management and insurance.
- Explain how classification trees are used to analyze risk management and insurance data.
- Explain how linear functions are used to analyze risk management and insurance data.
- Explain how cluster analysis is used to segment risk management and insurance data.

Outline

Traditional Analysis Techniques for Big Data

3

TRADITIONAL DATA ANALYSIS TECHNIQUES

Insurers and risk managers have long relied on traditional data analysis techniques to inform critical decisions, such as determining insurance rates and claims reserves. These techniques remain crucial to solving business problems, but they also form the foundation of newer methods.

Usually, traditional data analysis is used to determine one of these types of outcomes:

- A nonnumerical category into which data belongs—For example, an insurer may want to know whether an auto accident involves injuries or only property damage, or a risk manager may want to know whether certain employees have had an accident.
- A numerical answer based on data—For example, an insurer may want to analyze the data an applicant enters online to determine the premium for auto insurance.
- A probability score based on historical data—For example, a risk manager may want to determine the probability that a safety solution will reduce accident frequency, or an insurer may want to determine the probability of a commercial insured's having a catastrophic loss.
- A prediction of future results based on current and past data—For example, an insurer may want to determine the ultimate cost of claims for a line of insurance, or a risk manager may want to estimate the ultimate cost of employees' back injuries.

Traditional data analysis techniques include exploratory data analysis, **classification trees**, **regression analysis**, and **cluster analysis**. These techniques are usually applied to structured data, such as loss cost by claimant and type of injury. Sometimes, external structured data is also used, such as gross domestic product by month.

Classification tree
A supervised learning technique that uses a structure similar to a tree to segment data according to known attributes to determine the value of a categorical target variable.

Regression analysis
A statistical technique that is used to estimate relationships between variables.

Cluster analysis
A model that determines previously unknown groupings of data.

Exploratory Data Analysis

Exploratory data analysis is a valuable approach to a business problem that can be used before developing and testing a model. Through it, the analyst can develop a basic understanding of the data. The analyst can also obtain information about missing or inaccurate data.

The techniques used for exploratory data analysis are relatively simple. They involve charts and graphs that show data patterns and correlations among data. For example, a scatter plot, which is a two-dimensional plot of point values, could show the relationship between two attributes, such as driver age and average accident frequency. A bubble plot is a type of scatter plot in which the size of the bubble represents a third attribute for which there is data. An insurer, for example, may want to determine average accident severity in addition to average accident frequency by driver age. See the exhibit "Bubble Plot: Average Accident Frequency and Severity by Driver Age."

Bubble Plot: Average Accident Frequency and Severity by Driver Age

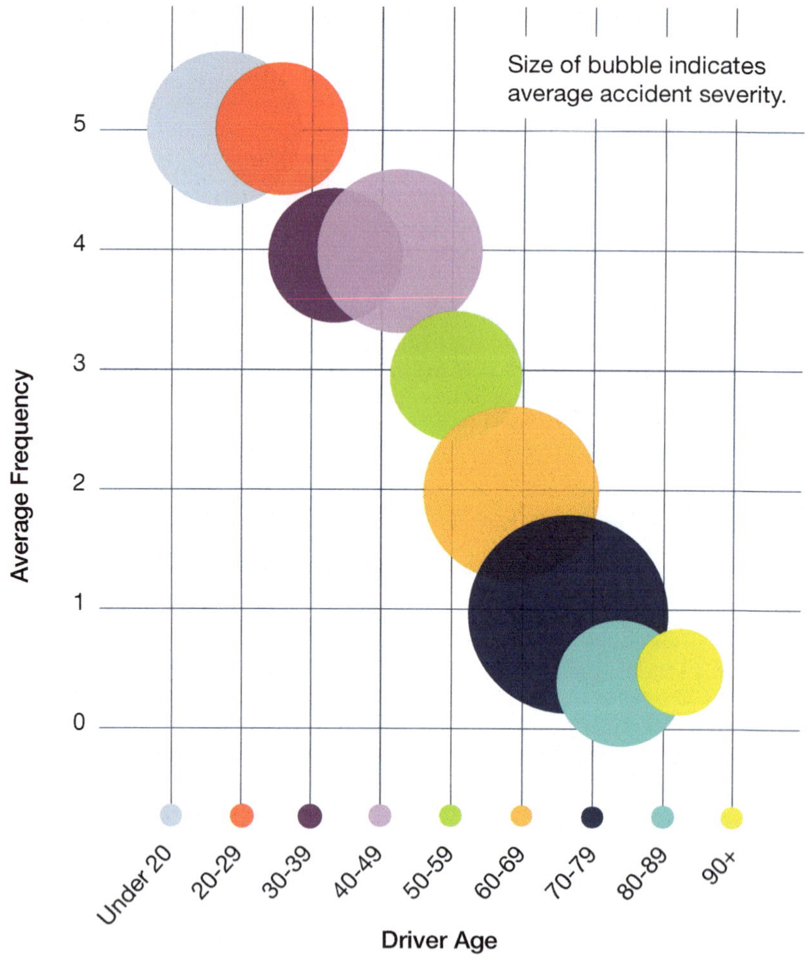

[DA12022]

A correlation matrix is another type of exploratory data analysis technique. For example, a risk manager identified a few worker attributes and would like to know whether they indicate that an employee is likely to work safely. The risk manager would like to develop a predictive model to identify the attributes of employees who are most likely to have an accident. These attributes can be explored using a correlation matrix. The stronger the correlation, the darker the cell's color in the matrix. The matrix indicated that certain combinations of attributes correlate strongly with worker accidents. Having had a prior accident in combination with certain other attributes, such as variable shifts, wage rates, and overtime, is particularly strongly correlated with worker accidents. See the exhibit "Data Analysis Techniques and Predictive Models."

Data Analysis Techniques and Predictive Models

After the analyst completes the exploratory data analysis and decides to develop a predictive model, he or she then selects the most appropriate technique for a model that will fit the business context and the type and source of the data. Like data and technology in general, these techniques continually evolve. However, a few are typically used, which can be adapted for each situation. For example, segmentation is used in both supervised and unsupervised learning techniques.

Most techniques employ machine learning, whereby a computer will continually refine the model as additional data and results are received. For example, association rule learning involves unsupervised learning in which a computer uses various algorithms to find potentially useful relationships among large amounts of data and to develop a rule that can be applied to new data.

When people shop online, the retailer often uses association rule learning to recommend additional products. For example, if someone purchases a book about computers, the retailer may send follow-up emails recommending additional computer books. Likewise, when a person has selected an item to purchase and is checking out, the retailer may recommend a similar item that is on sale before the purchase is finalized. Insurers may use association rule learning to recommend an umbrella policy, for example, when a customer purchases auto and homeowners insurance online.

[DA12696]

The risk manager then observed the correlations between the attribute of worker experience and the attributes of shift and overtime separately. The more-experienced employees usually work rotating shifts to ensure that an experienced employee is always present. Additionally, they are given preference for overtime work. Because experienced employees work variable shifts and long hours, they may be tired and therefore prone to accidents. As a result of this exploratory analysis, the risk manager realized that she should consult with human resources about workers' overtime and shift assignments before attempting to develop a predictive model. See the exhibit "Correlation Matrix: Attributes of Worker Safety."

Classification Trees

To solve business problems using data analysis, the data used must usually have certain relevant characteristics. For example, if a risk manager wants to

Correlation Matrix: Attributes of Worker Safety

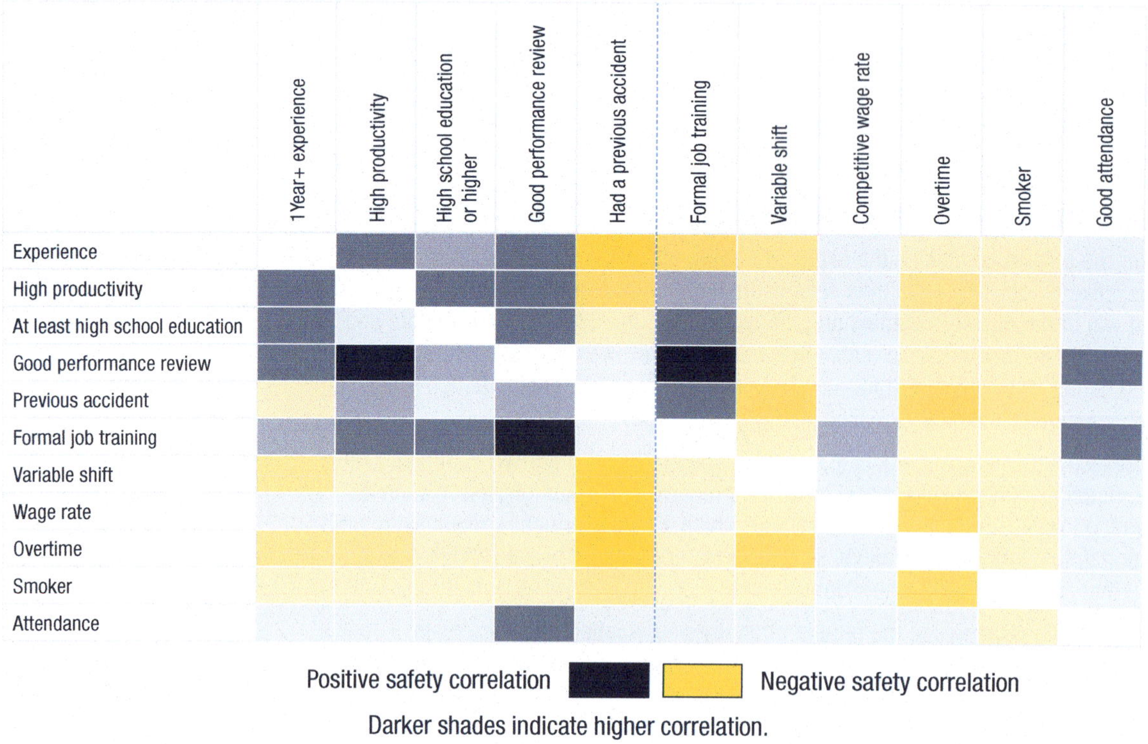

[DA12001]

determine whether an employee is likely to be able to return to work after an accident, the attributes used might include type of occupation, age, qualifications for retraining, and available positions with lighter physical requirements.

In this example, a classification tree could be used to segment workers compensation data. The tree would contain nodes, arrows, and leaf nodes. The leaf nodes of the tree indicate the values of the target variable. Each worker's attributes would follow the arrows of the tree through leaf nodes that segment the data by attribute to an ultimate leaf node labeled "Return to work" or "No return to work." It is important to understand that these classifications are not necessarily what the actual outcomes will be.

Regression Analysis

Linear regression
A statistical method to predict the numerical value of a target variable based on the values of explanatory variables.

In many cases, insurance or risk management professionals want to determine a numerical value for a target variable rather than, as in the previous example, a categorical value. In these cases, analysts use mathematical functions, such as those used in statistical regression techniques, to create algorithms. One of these methods is **linear regression**.

For example, a claims manager wants to determine the relationship between two attributes—the number of claims in a claims representative's caseload and his or her number of years of experience as a claims representative—and the target variable. Training and holdout data, the attribute values and target variable of which are known, is used to develop and test the model. Because the target variable is numerical, the analyst uses linear regression as the algorithm. The analyst develops this algorithm using a method that minimizes errors, represented by the differences between the actual target-variable values in the data and those forecast by the model.

Another type of linear model that can be used for more complex data classification is a **generalized linear model**. (This should not be confused with a general linear model, which is a broad group of different types of linear models.) A generalized linear model contains three components. The first is a random component, which refers to the probability distribution of the response variable. The second is a systematic component, which describes the linear combination of explanatory variables (attributes). The third component is a **link function**, which relates the results of the random and systematic components.

Generalized linear model (GLM)

A statistical technique that increases the flexibility of a linear model by linking it with a nonlinear function.

Link function

A mathematical function that describes how the random values of a target variable depend on the mean value generated by a linear combination of the explanatory variables (attributes).

Cluster Analysis

Cluster analysis is a technique for unsupervised learning. This technique is commonly used when an insurer knows a general problem it wants to solve but does not know the variables it must analyze to do so. For example, an insurer might want to determine the characteristics that increase claims severity so that it can assign claims that are likely to become severe to the most appropriate resources as soon as possible. The data analyst would develop a model to analyze a dataset of the insurer's severe claims. The results may show a clustering of claims around particular values of explanatory variables. For example, there might be a cluster of general liability claims around both claimants of a certain age and accidents that occur in a certain month. The analyst could then apply the information gained through cluster analysis to develop a predictive model using one of the other data analysis techniques that employ supervised learning.

CLASSIFICATION TREES

Research shows that a significant number of insurers analyze their data using decision trees, another term for classification trees, and use big data to assist in making underwriting decisions. Insurers have also embraced the use of predictive analytics to detect fraud. Additionally, the combination of analytics techniques and machine learning has enhanced insurers' predictive modeling capabilities.[1]

Because classification trees are widely used, it is important for risk management and insurance professionals to understand how they are used to analyze data and make predictions from the data.

Classification trees are a supervised learning technique. They are typically employed for problems with categorical answers—for example, predicting whether an insured will renew a policy. This type of answer is referred to as the target variable. Known attributes are used in the model to determine the category for the target variable.

Classification Tree Model

To illustrate the use of a classification tree, assume that an insurer would like to develop a model to determine at time of first report whether an uninsured motorists claim is fraudulent. When developing a classification tree model, various attributes are independently analyzed for the information gain they provide in classifying an uninsured motorists claim as fraudulent or not fraudulent. The insurer used these attributes in developing the model:

- Serious bodily injury but minor property damage to the vehicle—Yes/No
- Police report—Yes/No
- Customer tenure—Less than one year/More than one year
- Only witnesses are relatives or friends of the insured—Yes/No
- Other vehicle fled the scene—Yes/No
- Ambulance called—Yes/No

The attributes were then ranked according to their information gain. See the exhibit "Information Gain From Attributes for Detecting Uninsured Motorists Claims Fraud."

Recursively
Successively applying a model.

A classification tree is then built, through an induction process whereby the computer **recursively** analyzes different splits on the value of the attributes in various sequences based on training data. The tree is then applied to holdout data to see whether it generalizes so as to make accurate predictions using data that was not included in its development. There is a risk that the tree might overfit the training data. In such cases, it will not produce useful results and will need to be pruned.

The tree shown is simplified for illustration purposes. In reality, it would be much more complex. Note that the sequence of attributes does not follow the relative information gain ranking of the attributes, which is often the case when the attributes are analyzed recursively to construct a tree. See the exhibit "Classification Tree for Detecting Uninsured Motorists Claims Fraud."

Root node
The first node in a classification tree.

Node
A representation of a data attribute.

In the exhibit, the **root node** represents the attribute (serious bodily injury claim with minor property damage) that provides the greatest information gain for determining the value of the target variable. The data is further segmented at each **node** in the tree. The nodes represent attributes, and the branches are labeled with the possible values for each attribute.

Information Gain From Attributes for Detecting Uninsured Motorists Claims Fraud

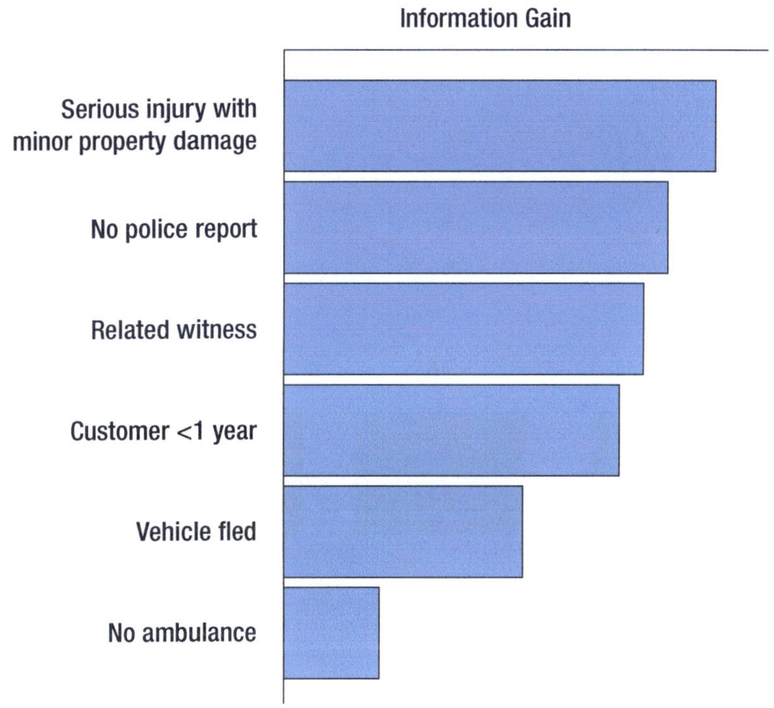

[DA12077]

At the root node, the data is segmented into "yes" for a serious claim with minor property damage and "no" for a serious claim with minor property damage. Then, a claim for serious injury with minor property damage continues down the right branch to the police report node (attribute). If the value of the police report node is "no" (no police report was filed), the claim then continues down to the customer tenure node. If the customer tenure value is "less than one year," the claim is classified as "fraud" at the **leaf node**. The exhibit shows three additional leaf nodes and their classification labels based on other combinations of node (attribute) values.

Leaf node
A terminal node of a classification tree that is used to classify an instance based on its attributes.

Classification Tree for Detecting Uninsured Motorists Claims Fraud

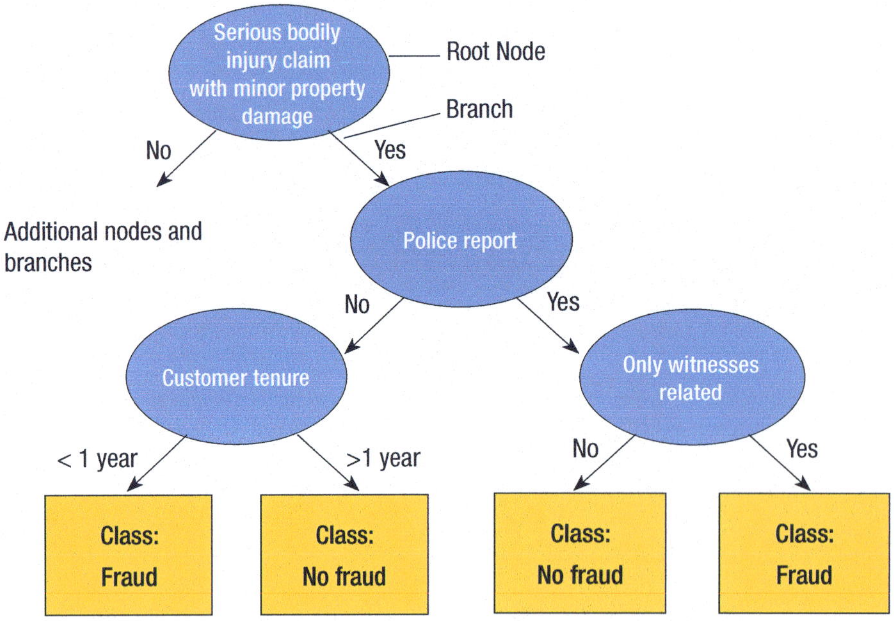

This illustration is a simplified version of a classification tree. It does not include all the attributes in the chart illustrating information gain. In actual practice, a classification tree model would be much more complex and include many more nodes.

[DA12078]

Classification Rules

From the classification tree, these rules for classifying new instances can be generated:

- An uninsured motorists claim with serious bodily injury and minor property damage, no police report, and customer tenure of less than one year is classified as "fraud."
- An uninsured motorists claim with serious bodily injury and minor property damage, no police report, and customer tenure of more than one year is classified as "no fraud."
- An uninsured motorists claim with serious bodily injury and minor property damage, a police report, and witnesses other than relatives of the insured is classified as "no fraud."
- An uninsured motorists claim with serious bodily injury and minor property damage, a police report, and only witnesses who are related to the insured is classified as "fraud."

Each classification rule is represented by a leaf (terminal) node of the classification tree.

It is important to note that claims classified as "fraud" are not necessarily fraudulent. The classification tree is indicating that they should be investigated further for possible fraud.

Probability Estimation Tree

Often, more information is desired than that provided by a simple classification. Users of predictive models want to know not only the predicted class for a new instance but also the likelihood, or probability, that it is correctly classified. This information enables them to do a cost-benefit analysis. For example, it helps them to determine which resources to devote to a claim based on the probability of its being correctly classified as fraudulent.

The data used to construct a classification tree can be used to estimate a probability. This is known as tree-based class probability estimation.

Tree-based probabilities are calculated by dividing the number of times the model correctly predicted the value of the target variable by the number of total predictions for each class at each leaf node. For example, assume that the model classifies 500 instances from the training data as fraudulent based on these attributes: an uninsured motorist claim with serious bodily injury and minor property damage, no police report, and customer tenure of less than one year. However, the actual number of fraudulent instances with these attribute values from the training data is 300, leaving 200 false positives produced by the model. The probability that the classification produced by the leaf node is correct is 300/500, or 60 percent. The probabilities that the classifications are correct for the other leaf nodes can be calculated in a similar manner. See the exhibit "Probability Estimation Tree."

The probabilities that instances falling into either of the two "no fraud" classes were correctly classified are .95 and .90, respectively. These probabilities are not unusual for a fraud prediction model; one would expect the vast majority of claims to be legitimate. The probabilities that instances falling into either of the two "fraud" categories were correctly classified are .60 and .55, respectively.

With machine learning, as this model is continually applied using new claims, it will respond to the new information and refine the classifications and their related probabilities.

When fraud is estimated based on data analytics, insurers should be aware of an increased risk of fraud but should also avoid jumping to conclusions in a given claim. Also, fraud investigations should comply with state and federal privacy laws. Nothing surpasses the value of a good investigation in determining the validity of a claim.

Probability Estimation Tree

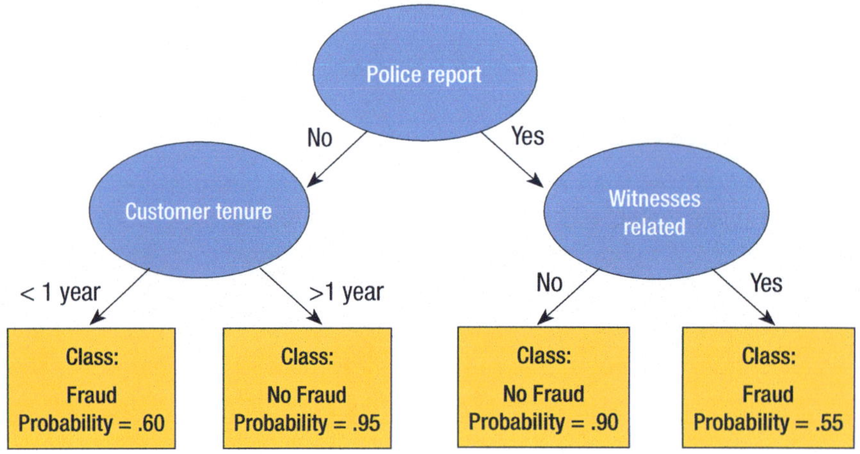

[DA12079]

LINEAR FUNCTIONS

Insurance and risk management professionals frequently encounter business situations in which predictive models can help them make decisions. For example, in deciding whether to underwrite a commercial account, an insurer may seek an estimate of whether the account will be profitable. And a risk manager may wish to estimate the likelihood that losses will exceed a certain amount to determine how much excess insurance to purchase.

Linear function
A mathematical model in which the value of one variable changes in direct proportion to the change in the value of another variable.

To aid these efforts, it is important for risk management and insurance professionals to understand how **linear functions** are used in models to predict various outcomes. Linear functions are graphed as straight lines. Accordingly, the equation for a linear function is the same as the equation for a straight line:

$y = mx + b$, where

y = the function (fx), the dependent variable

m = the slope of the line

x = the independent variable

b = the y-intercept (the point at which the line crosses the y-axis)

Linear discriminant
A data analysis technique that uses a line to separate data into two classes.

If an insurance or risk management professional wants to separate data into classes for prediction purposes, a **linear discriminant** function can be used. The boundary formed by this function is used to classify the data.

Alternatively, to forecast a numerical target variable as a function of explanatory variables, regression analysis is used. For example, an auto underwriter might want to predict the number of claims as a function of miles driven.

There are various types of regression analyses. The more commonly used are linear regression, generalized linear models, and **logistic regression**.

Logistic regression
A type of generalized linear model in which the predicted values are probabilities.

Linear Discriminants

A linear discriminant can be illustrated through an example. Suppose an insurer increases rates by 15 percent for a line of coverage and wants to predict which customers will not renew their policies after this increase. To develop a model, the insurer's data scientists identify attributes that are correlated with a customer's decision not to renew, which in this case are number of years as a customer and number of policies with the insurer. For illustration purposes, only two attributes are used. In reality, many more attributes would be used for a model of this type.

The data scientists assemble a dataset of customers who did and did not renew in a past year after a 15 percent rate increase, with all other conditions, such as market competitiveness, the same as with the current environment. For each customer, the values of the attributes and the target variable ("did not renew" or "renewed" the policy) are known. To train the model, the data scientists plot the data in an **instance space** and calculate a linear discriminant that best separates it into the two categories of the target variable. See the exhibit "Instance Space With Linear Discriminant—Policy Renewal Based on a 15% Premium Increase."

Instance space
An area of two or more dimensions that illustrates the distribution of instances.

Each instance (example) is plotted based on the values of its attributes. The known value of the target variable for each instance is indicated with a black dot for "did not renew" and a plus sign for "renewed." For illustration purposes, the number of instances (examples) is limited to twenty-five. In reality, many more instances would be used for a model of this type.

If more than two attributes are used, which is usually the case, the instance space would take on added dimensions. For example, with three attributes, the instance space would be a three-dimensional cube and the discriminant a plane rather than a line.

The linear discriminant separates the instances into the two classes. Note that it misclassifies some of the past instances. Two customers who fall below the linear discriminant actually renewed their policies, and three customers who fall above the linear discriminant did not renew their policies. These misclassifications need to be taken into account when evaluating the model's accuracy and precision.

Support vector machine
A linear discriminant that includes a margin on each side of the line for classifying data.

A **support vector machine (SVM)** is a technique often used to increase the accuracy of a linear discriminant. Note that the linear discriminant shown could have been drawn at different angles while still separating the data into the two classes. For example, the linear discriminant could have been drawn

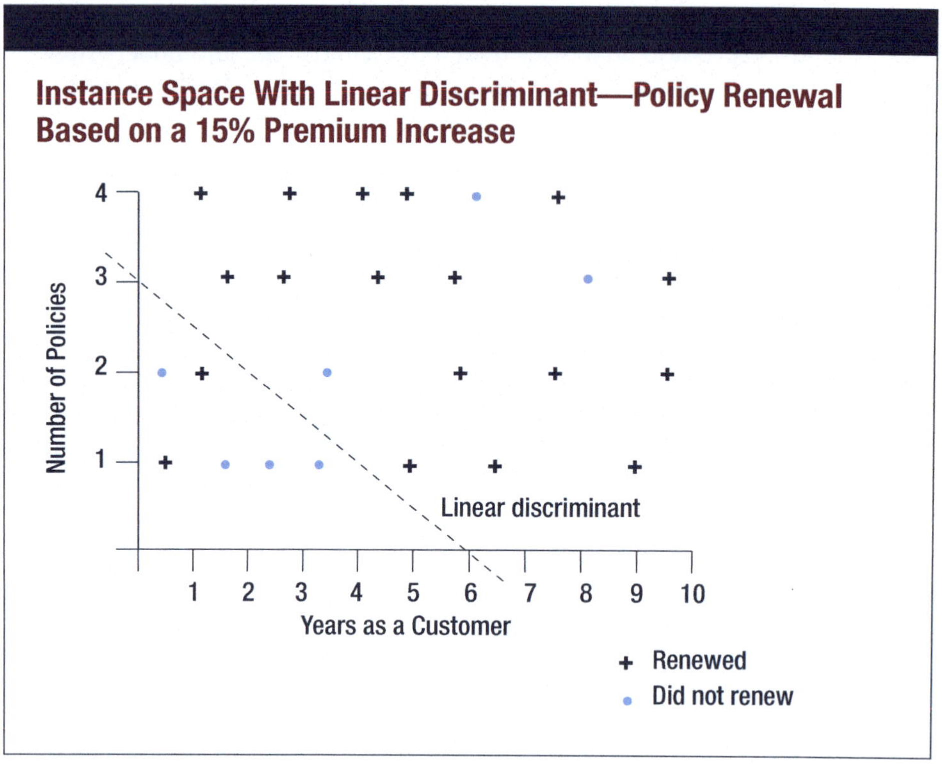

[DA12075]

to intersect the *x* axis at 5.5 years and the *y* axis at 4 years to separate the classes. An SVM adds a margin on each side of the discriminant line. It then applies mathematical equations to maximize the margins while selecting the optimal angle for the linear discriminant. This technique improves the accuracy of the linear discriminant in separating the classes.

The insurer uses the optimized linear discriminant to create rules to predict which of its current customers will or will not renew with a premium increase of 15 percent. These are the classification rules for the predictive model:

- If a customer instance falls above the linear discriminant, the customer is classified as "will renew."
- If a customer instance falls on or below the linear discriminant, the customer is classified as "will not renew."

The above rules are usually expressed as a mathematical function of the customer attribute values.

Linear Regression

Linear regression is another type of linear function that is widely used in predictive modeling. Unlike a linear discriminant, which is used to predict a class for the target variable, linear regression predicts a numerical value for the target variable as a function of one or more attributes (explanatory variables).

Furthermore, it assumes that the predicted value changes proportionately (a linear relationship) with the attribute values.

A safety professional might use linear regression to determine whether a linear relationship exists between a worker's years of experience (attribute) and the worker's number of safety violations in a year (target variable). An underwriter of motor vehicle fleets might use linear regression to determine whether a linear relationship exists among number of miles driven (attribute), driver experience (attribute), and frequency of accidents (target variable).

Just as with a linear discriminant, linear regression can be shown as a line on a two-dimensional graph. The value of the attribute (explanatory variable) is measured on the *x* axis and the value of the target variable on the *y* axis.

The exhibit shows a linear regression with number of years as a customer as the attribute (explanatory variable). The target variable is the policy renewal rate, which is calculated as the number of policies renewed divided by the total number of policies. The instances, or observations, which are used as training data to build the model, are shown as dots. Linear regression analysis is used to calculate a line that best fits the observations in order to estimate the mean relationship between the attribute and the target variable. See the exhibit "Linear Regression—Number of Years as a Customer and Policy Renewal Rates."

Linear Regression—Number of Years as a Customer and Policy Renewal Rates

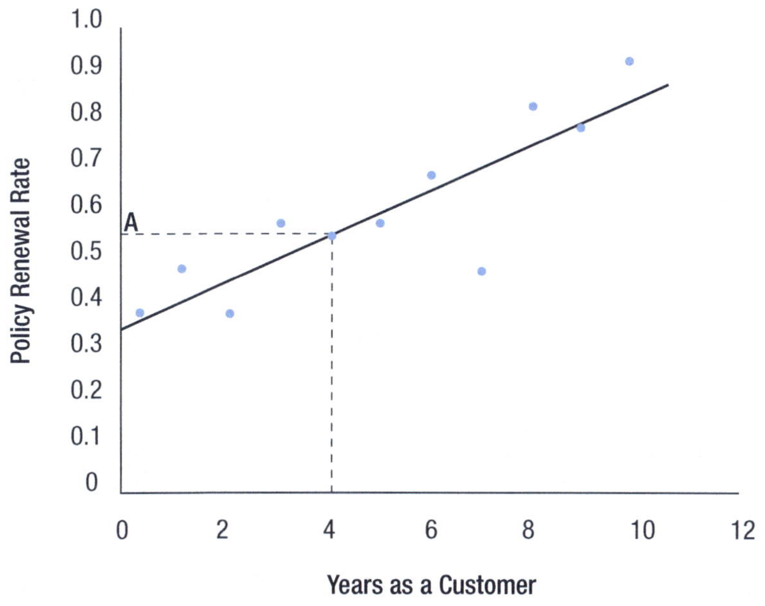

[DA09613]

For example, for customers who have been with the insurer for four years, the model estimates the mean policy renewal rate as 0.56, or 56 percent, as shown with the lines and with point A in the exhibit. Note that this is a simplified example; in reality, a renewal-rate prediction would be based on several attributes.

The vertical distances between the dots and the line are known as "errors" produced by the model. They are measured as the difference between observed value of the target variable (the dot) and the mean value as estimated by the line. In the example, the model estimated a mean value of 0.56 for the policy renewal rate. The actual observed value was 0.50, an error of 0.06.

Least squares regression

A type of linear regression that minimizes the sum of the squared values of the errors based on the differences between actual observed and estimated (mean) values.

Multiple regression

A variation of linear regression whereby two or more attributes (explanatory variables) are used for prediction.

The objective in calculating the regression line is to minimize total errors. A common algorithm for determining the line minimizes the sum of the squared errors and is known as **least squares regression**. Squaring the errors increases the penalty for values further from the line compared with those closer to the line.

Multiple Regression

If a single attribute does not sufficiently explain changes in the target variable, **multiple regression** can be performed to introduce additional attributes. In the example, "number of policies with the insurer" could be added as a second attribute. The regression line would sit in a three-dimensional space with the values of the second attribute plotted along the third dimension.

In calculating the multiple regression line, the value of each attribute would be weighted based on its influence in estimating the value of the target variable. For example, policy renewal rate (the target variable) might be expressed as follows:

Policy renewal rate = 0.08 x number of years as a customer + 0.03 x number of policies, with 0.08 and 0.03 serving as weights of each of the attributes, respectively.

Disadvantages of Linear Models

Linear models, including linear regression, have these disadvantages when applied to property-casualty insurance:

Homoskedasticity

In linear modeling, variance of the model errors around the estimated mean of the target variable is the same regardless of its size.

- They assume that the variability (as measured by the model errors), or variance, around the estimated mean of the target variable is normally distributed and therefore follows a standard symmetrical pattern. With property-casualty insurance data, variability around the mean is not normally distributed.
- They also assume that variability around the estimated mean of the target variable is the same regardless of its size. This is known as **homoskedasticity**. With property-casualty insurance data, the variability around an estimated mean of the target variable usually varies with its size.

Generalized Linear Models

A generalized linear model (GLM) helps overcome the limitations of linear models, including linear regression. Just as its name implies, a GLM generalizes a linear model to increase its flexibility in modeling relationships between attributes (explanatory variables) and the target variable. GLMs are widely used in the property-casualty insurance business.

These are characteristics of GLMs:

- GLMs use a link function that defines the relationship between the mean values estimated by a linear model (called the systematic component) and the variability of the target variable around those means (called the random component).
- The random component is usually specified as an exponential distribution, which is not normally distributed. This overcomes the problem previously discussed that the random component of a linear model is normally distributed.
- The variability (variance) of an exponential distribution is a function of its mean, overcoming the problem of homoskedasticity.

An example helps illustrate the application of a GLM. When estimating auto claims frequency, it is common to use a linear model of various explanatory variables, such as miles driven and driver experience, as the systematic component. The mean values estimated by the linear model are connected with a log link function to a **Poisson distribution**, an exponential distribution that serves as the random component. A Poisson distribution is commonly used to model a probability distribution of claims frequency.

Poisson distribution
A distribution providing the probability of a number of independent events happening in a fixed time period.

Logistic Regression

Insurance and risk management professionals often use classification analysis to determine the value of a binary target variable. For example, an insurer may want to know whether, based on his or her characteristics, a current policyholder should be classified as "will renew" or "will not renew." A risk manager may want to know whether, based on its characteristics, a claim should be classified as "fraudulent" or "not fraudulent."

However, users of predictive models often want to know not only the predicted class for a new instance (for example, a policyholder or a claim), but also the likelihood, or probability, that it falls into that class. For example, the insurer may want to know the probability that a customer who is classified as "will not renew" will not actually renew his or her policy. This is known as **class probability estimation** and is accomplished through logistic regression.

Class probability estimation
An estimate of the probability that an instance will fall into its predicted class.

Logistic regression is a type of generalized linear model that uses a link function based on the logarithm of the odds (log odds, or logit) of the event occurring. (The odds of an event occurring is the ratio of the probability of the event occurring to the probability of the event not occurring.) The log odds are then translated into a probability that the event of interest, such as policy nonrenewal, actually falls into its predicted class. Common transactions are based on logistic regression. For example, when a customer applies for auto insurance, a logistic regression model is used to decide whether to accept the applicant.

CLUSTER ANALYSIS

There are times when insurers and risk managers would like to obtain more information, but they do not know the precise nature of that information. For example, an insurer may want to know more about its customers to select the best marketing techniques for different customer segments. A risk manager may want to compare characteristics of its fleet drivers. In these situations, data analytics techniques that use known variables will not be effective. Cluster analysis is a technique that can explore data to discover previously unknown information or relationships. Risk management and insurance professionals should understand how clustering can explore data to provide new information.

There are different methods of cluster analysis that segment data according to similarities in various attributes. Several iterations of cluster analysis can be applied to subdivide clusters and provide more granular information. For example, if an insurer has identified segments of its customers according to age, it may want to explore millennial customers to identify characteristics that could provide insight into products and marketing approaches that might interest this group.

This discussion uses an example to explain how different methods of cluster analysis can be used to segment data. The example provides an understanding of how the segmentation can then provide relevant information that can be used to guide business decisions.

Cluster Analysis

In this example, the risk manager of a large organization works with a data science team to discover additional information about employee injuries. The data scientist uses cluster analysis on data regarding employees who have had injuries. Cluster analysis is an unsupervised learning technique in which the data scientist will explore and evaluate clusters of particular characteristics.

The initial cluster analysis segmented the employee injuries into two large clusters. One cluster included employees who returned to work, and the other cluster included employees who did not return to work. The risk manager decided to discover the characteristics of the injured employees who did not return to work. By analyzing these characteristics, the risk manager could consider transitional duty assignments that might assist these employees in returning to the workforce.

Hierarchical Clustering

One type of cluster analysis is **hierarchical clustering.** The hierarchical groups can be represented by circles within circles. The circles in the illustration represent these clusters of attributes of injured employees who did not return to work:

Hierarchical clustering
A modeling technique in which multiple clusters are grouped according to their similarities.

- Circle 1 includes all the claims in which the injured employee did not return to work.
- Circle 2 includes all the claims in which the employee had a prior significant injury or medical condition.
- Circle 3 includes all the claims in which the employee has a medium- to heavy-duty occupation.
- Circle 4 includes all back injuries.
- Circle 5 includes all knee injuries.
- Circle 6 includes all types of multiple injuries (for example, arm and ankle).

The points within the circles indicate individual instances within the clusters of data. The circles represent ways of grouping the individual data points according to similarity. The largest circles form the largest groups, or clusters, of data. See the exhibit "Hierarchical Clustering."

The clusters labeled in the hierarchical clustering illustration can then be grouped according to their distance from each other. A **dendogram** is frequently used to present the groups of clusters obtained from the hierarchical clustering. If clusters are grouped at one level of the hierarchy, they remain grouped at each higher level. The distance between clusters represents how similar each cluster is to another cluster.

Dendogram
A diagram that illustrates the groupings from hierarchical clustering.

G, for example, represents an instance that is a significant distance from clusters or groups and is therefore an outlier. Its characteristics would have to be explored to determine its relevance. For example, if G represents a claim in which a paper cut became infected, it could be disregarded as an isolated instance. F is an instance within the circle containing claims in which the employee had a preexisting injury or medical condition. If F represents a claim for a paper cut that became infected, it may need to be explored to determine whether the underlying medical condition—for example, diabetes—predisposed the claimant to an infection. See the exhibit "Dendogram."

K Nearest Neighbors Algorithm

Hierarchical clustering organizes instances and clusters according to similarities. A different way to use clustering is to employ a k nearest neighbor (k-NN) technique. The data science team can apply this technique to the data on all employees who have had workplace injuries to determine the value of characteristics of those who did or did not return to work. In a simple example, if a new claim's five nearest neighbors in a dataset did not return

Hierarchical Clustering

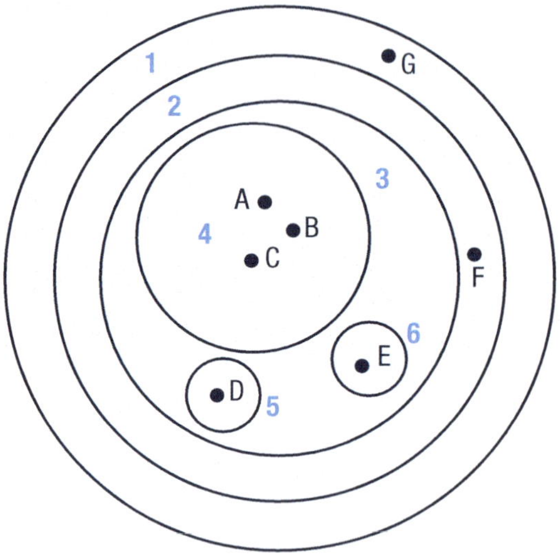

1 = All
2 = Prior/Significant Injury/Medical Condition
3 = Medium- to Heavy-Duty Occupation
4 = Back Injury
5 = Knee Injury
6 = Multiple Injuries

[DA12051]

to work, it could be predicted that the new claim is also likely to involve an employee who will probably not return to work. In another example, if three of the nearest neighbors involved employees who did not return to work and two involved employees who did return to work, it could be predicted that the new claim would also involve an employee who is unlikely to return to work because of the results of a majority of its neighbors. This is the voting method. In another method, the average of the claims in which the employee did not return to work could be used, which equals 3/5 or 0.6. The new claim would have a probability score of 0.6 for the employee not returning to work.

An important issue in k-NN is what number k should equal. In general, the higher the number of k, the more accurate the prediction is likely to be. This is because the prediction is based on more data. However, an even more accurate method for k-NN is to weigh the value of each distance based on its similarity to a new claim. The nearest neighbors, those that are most similar, would have the greatest weight. With this method, although k should be large enough to consider a representative sample of claims, the issue of how large k should be becomes less important.

Dendogram

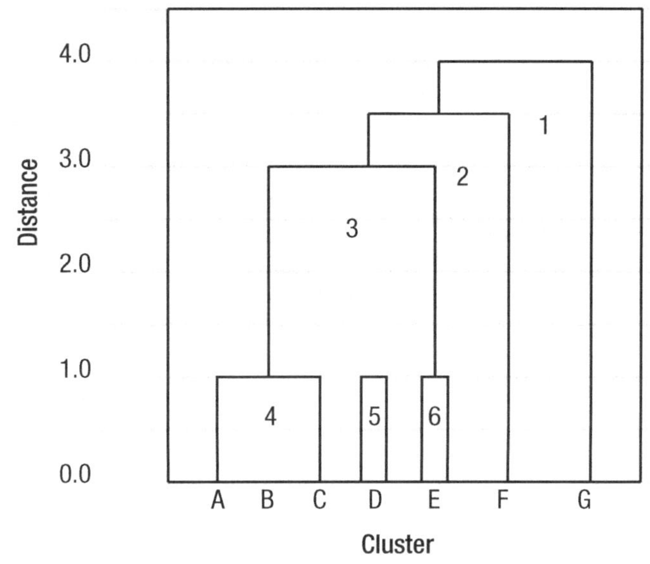

[DA12052]

K-Means Clustering Algorithm

Another clustering technique that uses nearest neighbors is **k-means**. The **centroid** is the average of the values for the instances in each cluster.

The risk manager wants to know whether an employee's age affects whether the employee returns to work. The data scientist applies a k-means cluster algorithm to the data regarding all injured employees. Each cluster represents ages of employees. The centroid represents the average age and the average percentage of the employees in the cluster who returned to work. See the exhibit "K-Means Cluster."

K-means

An algorithm in which "k" indicates the number of clusters and "means" represents the clusters' centroids.

Centroid

The center of a cluster.

Describing Clusters

Because clustering techniques are unsupervised, it is important to understand what type of information can be learned from them. In a supervised learning data analysis technique, the target variable is known. In clustering analysis, the target variable is unknown.

There are two types of descriptions for clusters:

- A characteristic description describes the typical attributes of the cluster.
- A differential description describes the differences between the instances of one cluster and those of other clusters.

K-Means Cluster

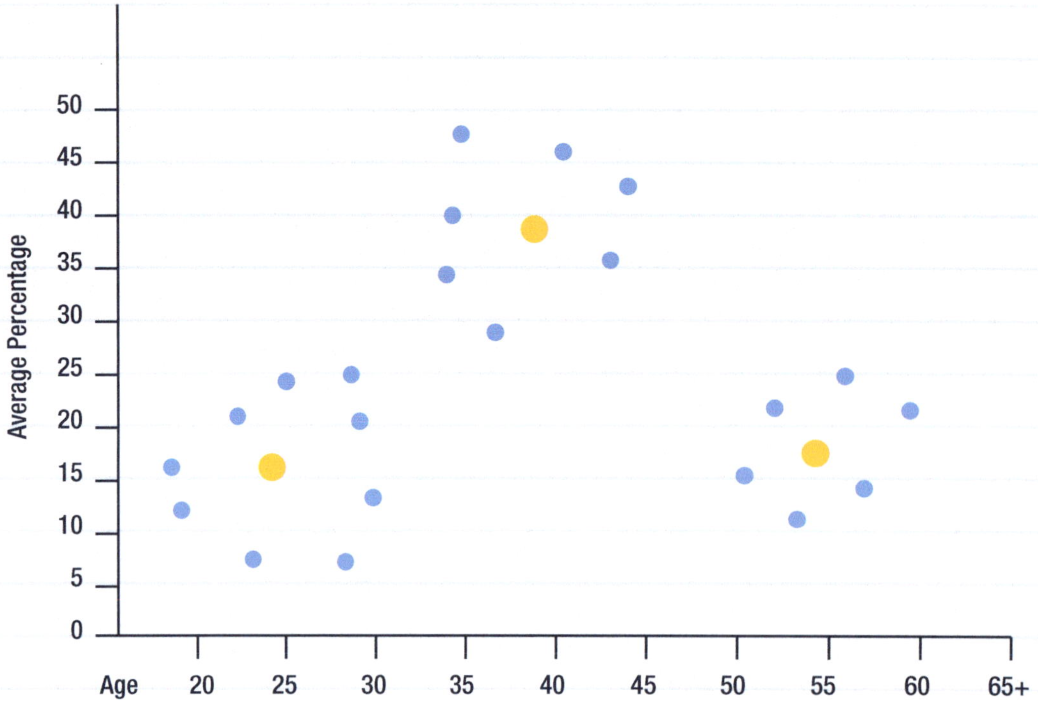

[DA12053]

In the examples discussed, the hierarchical clustering for claims involving employees who did not return to work presented a characteristic description of these employees. The claims were clustered into groups according to similar attributes, such as whether the employee had a prior injury or medical condition. The k-means clustering presented a differential description. The clustering around different characteristic points provided attributes that were different for each cluster in order to distinguish those claims in which the employee did not return to work from those in which the employee did return to work.

SUMMARY

Traditional data analysis techniques remain crucial to solving business problems, but they also form the foundation of newer methods. These techniques include exploratory data analysis, classification trees, various types of statistical regression models, and cluster analysis.

For risk management and insurance purposes, a classification tree is a useful data analysis technique for predicting a categorical result. For example, to help determine which claims warrant additional fraud investigation, a classification tree model can segment claims into classes according to values of various combinations of attributes. Additionally, the tree can be used to calculate the probability that a claim with those attributes will be correctly classified. The output of the classification tree helps the insurer determine which claims should be referred for additional fraud investigation.

A linear discriminant can be used to classify data and generate classification rules for a target variable based on attributes. Regression analysis can be used to forecast a numerical target variable based on attributes, and linear regression is widely used for predictive models. Generalized linear modeling is more flexible than linear regression and helps overcome its limitations. Logistic regression, a type of generalized linear modeling, is used for class probability estimation, which determines the probability that an event that falls into the target class will occur.

Cluster analysis is an unsupervised learning technique that is useful for exploring data. The three most common types of clustering are hierarchical, k nearest neighbor, and k-means. A clustering algorithm can be applied in several iterations to obtain more granular attributes of data for various purposes, such as learning more about customers or developing a predictive model. It is important to understand the results of cluster analysis. The two major ways to interpret the results are characteristic description and differential description.

ASSIGNMENT NOTE

1. Klayton Southwood and J.J. Ihrke, "P&C Insurers' Big Data Aspirations for Advanced Predictive Analytics," Willis Towers Watson, February 2016, www.towerswatson.com/en-US/Insights/Newsletters/Americas/americas-insights/2016/pc-insurers-big-data-aspirations-for-advanced-predictive-analytics (accessed April 15, 2016).

Direct Your Learning

4

Text Mining, Social Network Analysis, and Neural Networks

Educational Objectives

After learning the content of this assignment, you should be able to:

- Summarize text mining concepts and their application to risk management and insurance.
- Summarize social network analysis concepts and their application to risk management and insurance.
- Explain how neural networks are used to analyze risk management and insurance data.

Outline

Text Mining, Social Network Analysis, and Neural Networks

4

TEXT MINING

The sheer abundance of text available about customers, claims, and risks makes it an obvious source of data for risk managers and insurers investing in data mining. However, the text in claims files, social media posts, news stories, and consumer reviews is not automatically meaningful to a machine or an algorithm.

Text must be cleaned up and turned into structured data before it can be used in a model. To understand the challenges and benefits of text mining, it is important to understand its process. See the exhibit "The Text Mining Process."

The Text Mining Process

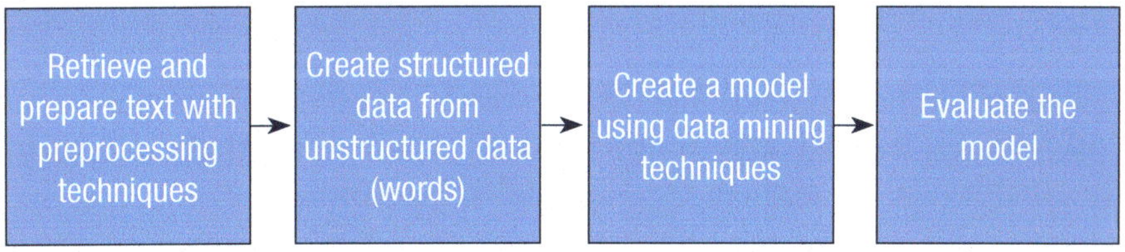

[DA12046]

Retrieve and Prepare Text

The first step in the text mining process is collecting a set of documents, which is called a **corpus**. A corpus is a group of related documents, such as a group of claims files or product reviews. A text document has no size restrictions—it may be a one-sentence social media comment or a fifty-page report.[1] Each document is made up of various words, also called terms or **tokens**.

Corpus

A collection of writings or documents.

Token

In a text mining context, a meaningful term or group of terms.

When text is retrieved, most is not clean enough to be of use for any type of modeling. Some people type in all capital or all lowercase letters, and misspellings and abbreviations are common. Additionally, many words in the English language provide little value in a text mining context, such as articles, conjunctions, and prepositions.

To turn unstructured data into structured data, several preprocessing steps are required:[2]

- Extract the words from the data, typically discarding spaces, punctuation, and numbers (depending on the context)
- Eliminate words that convey little or no information—for example, "and" and "the"
- Account for synonyms by creating a project-specific dictionary and for the **stemming** of words by removing their suffixes

Stemming

The removal of a suffix from a term for the purpose of text mining.

Consider this example of an excerpt from a claims file and note the words that need to be removed, flagged, or stemmed (punctuation and numbers are not flagged for readability). See the exhibit "Text Mining Claims Notes."

Text Mining Claims Notes

12/20/X1 Estimate~~s~~ rec'd ~~and~~ difference~~s~~ analyz~~ed~~ ~~to~~ ensure fair comparison. Call~~ed~~ ~~Mrs.~~ Darlington ~~and~~ review~~ed~~ repair estimate ~~with her~~. Agre~~ed~~ ~~on~~ settlement amount.
Process~~ed~~ payment today.
Close~~d~~ file.

[DA12047]

Stopword

A common word that offers little meaning and is filtered out in a text mining context.

A computer can be trained to ignore **stopwords**, recognize abbreviations, and remove suffixes. It can also be trained to look for the words that are relevant to the situation being studied; these are called keywords.

Create Structured Data From Unstructured Data

To apply a modeling algorithm to text, the text must be put into a form that the algorithm can recognize, such as by giving it numerical values.

From unstructured data, key terms can be extracted and represented in a table or spreadsheet. The table provides a means of labeling a document with familiar modeling terms; each document or each row in the table can be considered an instance (example), and each term or each column in the table can be considered an attribute.

Term frequency

A measurement of how often a term appears in a document.

A common approach to presenting structured data is to count the number of times each term appears in each document. **Term frequency** can help an analyst decide how important a term is in a particular context. Assume that the Text Mining Claims Note exhibit (Document 1) came from a corpus of similar claims documents. See the exhibit "Structured Data Results of Claims Files With Term Frequency."

Structured Data Results of Claims Files With Term Frequency

	Repair (repaired, repairing)	Estimat (estimate, estimated, estimating)	Auto (car)	Payment	Analyz (analyzed, analyzing, analyzes)	Settlement	Respon (responded, response)
Document (Claims File) 1	1	2	0	1	1	1	0
Document (Claims File) 2	3	1	1	2	1	2	3
Document (Claims File) 3	2	0	1	1	1	1	2
Count	6	3	2	4	3	4	5

[DA12048]

While the frequency, or count, of a term measures how many times that term appears in a document, how meaningful is that number? Overly common as well as rare terms have diminished value in a text mining context. For example, a homeowners insurer's claims files would most likely have a high occurrence of the word "home," but that fact would not give the insurer any new knowledge. In addition, if a claims representative noted that a homeowner works at a restaurant, the word "restaurant" would likely be rare in homeowners' claims files, but it is probably also insignificant. One way to account for this is to set upper and lower limits on term frequency and ignore terms that fall above or below those limits.[3]

Another way of examining term frequency is **inverse document frequency (IDF)**, which is measured in this way:

IDF(t) = 1 + log (Total number of documents/Number of documents containing t)

IDF can be thought of as a measure of a term's rarity within a corpus. The higher a term's IDF, the rarer the term is within a given corpus [and the more potentially meaningful it is to the document(s) it appears in]. For example, if many claims files in a corpus mention the word "fraud," the corpus is probably a collection of fraudulent claims files. Perhaps the insurer is looking for reasons for or signifiers of the fraud. Regardless, the term's frequency throughout the corpus indicates its insignificance for any one document. However, if only a few of the claims files mention fraud, the term becomes significant within the documents in which it is mentioned, and those files should be flagged. The fewer documents in which the term is mentioned, the more important it becomes to those documents (after eliminating extremely rare terms). See the exhibit "Sentiment Analysis."

Inverse document frequency (IDF)
The significance of a term within a document of text in a corpus based on how many documents within which it appears in that corpus.

Sentiment Analysis

Sentiment analysis is a way of measuring the opinion of something (often a product), be it positive, negative, or neutral. In sentiment analysis, each term is given a positive, negative, or neutral value. The values are added to produce a sentiment score. A challenge lies in the fact that a computer will not take context into account. For this reason, a sentiment analysis algorithm works best when it is developed for a particular purpose. For example, the term "cheap" could be viewed as positive in the context of reviewing an auto insurance premium, but it would most likely be seen as negative in the description of a replacement part for that auto.

[DA12049]

Create a Model Using Data Mining Techniques

Prepared and cleaned-up text can be used in a variety of models for both supervised and unsupervised learning. For example, suppose that an insurer has experienced a recent increase in the cost of its claims. By performing a cluster analysis on claims notes, the insurer may discover indicators of claims fraud.

The similarity of documents can be analyzed to discover which documents are nearest neighbors. Once a claim has been identified as fraudulent, the number of similar words between its file and other files can indicate the likelihood that the other claims are fraudulent.

A predictive model could then be built using the fraud-correlated terms as attributes. "Yes, fraudulent" and "no, not fraudulent" would be the class labels of the target variables. Using the preceding table of structured data as an example, by adding a column for the class label of the target variable, the same data can be used for a classification model. Training data in which the values of the class labels are known should be used to develop the model, which is then evaluated using holdout data.

By looking at the results of a classification model, rules can be created and applied to new documents. For example, suppose a company has an unusually high number of workers compensation claims and it suspects some of the employee claimants of fraud. After creating a model that monitors employee email and examining the results, the company could institute a rule that any employee who has recently filed for workers compensation benefits, has not returned to work for at least two weeks, and used the phrase "They owe me" in an interoffice email be investigated.

However, there are drawbacks to this approach. It can be difficult to find an exact phrase replicated across numerous text documents. It may be a coincidence that a certain phrase significantly appeared in the training data, and once the model is used in production, it may be the result of overfitting and being unable to apply generalization. The company may find that the term "owe" is a more consistent indicator of fraud. That word will undoubtedly appear in relation to nonfraudulent claims as well; for example, "I owe the doctor for my last visit." However, by reducing the string of words to one word, the model will now pick up on additional phrases, such as "This company owes me."

Continuing the example, the company may want to be able to predict the probability that the term "owe" will correlate with fraudulent workers compensation claims—essentially, how much information gain the term "owe" provides. After probability has been determined, a linear scoring method provides weight to each term, based on its probability, which appears in a document. The document is then given a final score, which is the probability that it indicates fraud.

In some text mining situations—particularly those involving large amounts of data and limited amounts of time—it can be beneficial to skip some of the preprocessing steps and have the computer itself find the meaningful words in unstructured data. One approach is to create a set of linguistic rules that can automatically process text; the results are represented as a **semantic network**. A second approach to text mining unstructured data is the use of **neural networks**. Neural networks attempt to replicate the thought process of the human brain; however, they have limitations in linguistic settings. New text mining techniques are attempting to combine these two approaches.[4]

Semantic network

A network that shows the logical relationships between concepts.

Neural network

A data analysis technique composed of three layers, including an input layer, a hidden layer with nonlinear functions, and an output layer, that is used for complex problems.

Evaluate the Text Mining Model

The effectiveness of a text mining model can be evaluated through traditional data-modeling performance metrics, such as accuracy, precision, recall, and F-score. However, accuracy is not the best measure of text applications because of the high number of negative results—for example, most words in claims notes will not correlate with fraudulent claims.[5]

Using a **confusion matrix** of the text mining results, the metrics can be calculated. The exhibit shows hypothetical numbers based on the example of fraudulent workers compensation claims being identified from the workers' interoffice emails that contain the term "owe." See the exhibit "Performance Metrics for Text Mining Example."

Confusion matrix

A matrix that shows the predicted and actual results of a model.

Performance Metrics for Text Mining Example

Out of 100 Emails	"Owe" Not Present	"Owe" Present
Not fraudulent	45 true negatives (*TN*)	15 false positives (*FP*)
Fraudulent	10 false negatives (*FN*)	30 true positives (*TP*)

Precision: $TP \div (TP + FP)$

$$30 \div (30 + 15) = 0.67$$

Recall: $TP \div (TP + FN)$

$$30 \div (30 + 10) = 0.75$$

F-score: $2 \times ([\text{Precision} \times \text{recall}] \div [\text{Precision} + \text{recall}])$

$$2 \times ([0.67 \times 0.75] \div [0.67 + 0.75]) = 0.71$$

[DA12050]

SOCIAL NETWORK ANALYSIS

Everyone is part of a social network, and scientists have been researching the effects of networks on psychology and diseases for years. With the prevalence of social media, more network connections exist than ever before. People on opposite sides of the world can connect through Facebook statuses, tweets, and countless other ways. But why should the mechanics of these connections matter to the business world, particularly to insurance and risk management professionals?

Insurance and risk management professionals need to understand their customers and the risks they represent so that they can better serve them. **Social network analysis**, a type of **network analysis**, provides a way to not only better understand individuals but also analyze how they are linked to and influenced by others.

Social network analysis

The study of the connections and relationships among people in a network.

Network analysis

The study of the nodes (vertices) and edges (lines) in a network.

These methods offer ways to observe social network connections:

- Link analysis
- Social network metrics
- Network classification

Introduction to Social Network Analysis

Although in today's society, the term "social network" immediately brings to mind social media, social network analysis applies to much more. Social network analysis is used in many fields, ranging from medicine, where it is applied to determine disease progression, to law enforcement, where it can help detect terror networks and crime rings. Social network analysis differs from other fields of data analysis because rather than focusing on the attributes of each node, or instance, it focuses on how those data points relate to others in the network.

A social network, such as the email communication among co-workers in an office, can be viewed as a **sociogram**. These graphs are particularly useful for analyzing small social networks. A sociogram, or network graph, is made up of **nodes (vertices)** and **edges**. When examining a sociogram, think of each node as an actor and each edge as a relationship. For example, each point is an employee, and each line is an email sent. See the exhibit "Simple Sociogram."

Sociogram

A graphic representation of a social network.

Node (vertex)

In network analytics, a point in a network.

Edge

A link in a network.

Simple Sociogram

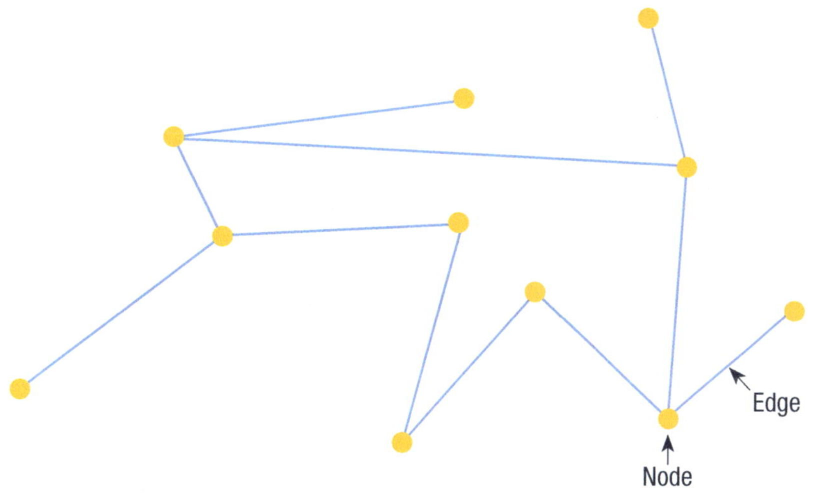

[DA12060]

Some graphs use arrows to distinguish that some connections are flowing in only one direction, and some use weighted edges (essentially, thicker or thinner lines) to show the strength or frequency of the connections. A **directed tie**, represented by an arrow, may or may not be reciprocated. For example, when people follow a celebrity on Twitter, the celebrity typically does not follow them. The relationship flows in one direction and would be represented by a line with one arrow. Differently colored nodes can be used to represent gender or status. See the exhibit "Directed and Weighted Sociogram."

Directed tie

An edge within a network graph that has direction.

A sociogram of a large network can quickly become difficult to follow, and the best way to analyze a larger social network is through a **matrix**.[6] The "Social Network Matrix" exhibit represents the same connections shown in the "Directed and Weighted Sociogram" exhibit, only now through rows and columns. Social distance is scored with a one for a relationship and a zero for the lack of a relationship. For simplicity, the weights of the connections are not considered in this matrix. See the exhibit "Social Network Matrix."

Matrix

In social network analysis, the representation of data through rows and columns.

Directed and Weighted Sociogram

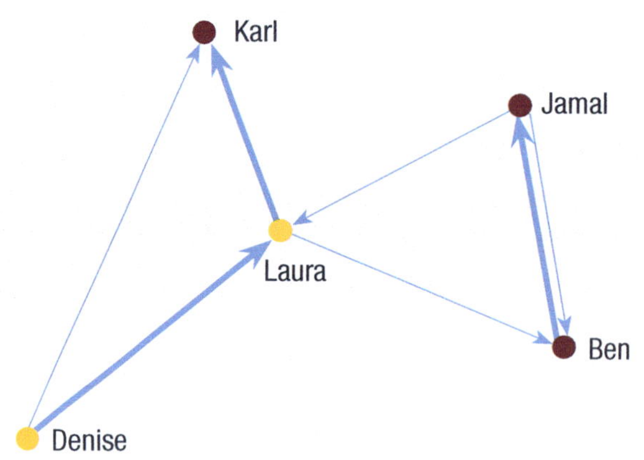

[DA12061]

Social Network Matrix

	Denise	Laura	Karl	Jamal	Ben
Denise		1	1	0	0
Laura	0		1	0	1
Karl	0	0		0	0
Jamal	0	1	0		1
Ben	0	0	0	1	

[DA12062]

Sentiment analysis
The process of determining the opinion or emotion behind a selection of text.

Data mining techniques can be used to analyze these networks. Both supervised learning techniques, such as classification, and unsupervised learning techniques, such as clustering, can be applied. One way of analyzing social networks involving text communication (such as social media networks) is through text mining. Examining the results of text mining in the context of a network gives them even more meaning. For example, a **sentiment analysis** is much more valuable when the study also considers how many people have read a particular sentiment. If a company is mining posts about a new product and is concerned about a high frequency of negative reviews, performing a network analysis to see how many people the negative reviewers are linked to would be worthwhile.

Link Analysis

Links are a key aspect of network analysis. A link is the connection between two people or between a person and a thing. For example, on Facebook, two people can be linked as "friends." Webpages often link to other webpages, and examining how many links lead to a particular webpage can provide a good analysis of the page's significance and of how many people it will reach. Links can be examined to determine who will likely influence whom and also how closely people and things are connected. For example, will information from Chloe travel to her co-worker first or to her sister? The person she communicates with more could be determined through link analysis.

Link prediction is the process of trying to predict a pair of links—for example, who will be friends or what movie someone will like. It can also be used to try to classify a link that is currently neutral by measuring similarity to other links and predicting whether a link will become positive (for example, a friendship or a purchase) or negative (for example, nonrenewal of a policy or subscription).

Measuring similarity, the basis of link prediction, allows insurance and risk management professionals to analyze groups of customers and/or potential customers and observe trends. For example, if a linked group of a producer's homeowners customers begins buying sailboats, the producer may want to recommend that the insurer offer these customers small boat policies.

Insurance and risk management professionals should be aware, though, that data mining of social media sites raises privacy concerns for many consumers and consumer advocates. When people make personal information publicly available, they typically do not expect it to be used in conjunction with bits of information about them from other sources to create in-depth profiles. Insurers should ensure that they are transparent in their use of social media, particularly when modeling social media data to make underwriting or rating changes.

Social Network Metrics

The flow of communication (or whatever is being analyzed) in a network can be examined in terms of "walks" from node to node. For example, a Facebook post may walk from the original poster to someone else who reposts it to the final reader. The term "path" is used to describe how something flows through a network, passing each node and edge only once.[7] The efficiency of the flow between social network connections can be determined through these **centrality measures**:[8]

Centrality measure
In a social network context, the quantification of a node's relationship to other nodes in the same network.

- Degree—A measure of the connections each node has. For example, degree would measure the number of external webpages the insurer's webpage links to or the number of Facebook friends one of the insurer's producers has.

- Closeness—The measure of the average distance, or path length, between a particular node and the other nodes in a network. For example, John and Anne both find out that a company policy is changing. Because Anne has a higher "closeness" to the company's other employees than does John, as measured through the company's email traffic, it is reasonable to assume that Anne will spread the news to more people more quickly through email than will John.
- Betweenness—The measure of how many times a particular node is part of the shortest path between two other nodes in a network. If a scholarly article is posted online and most of its readers click on one of its cited references, read the graduate thesis it cites, and then connect with the thesis's authors, the article has a high degree of betweenness because it connects two groups of people: the authors of the thesis and the readers of the scholarly article.

A kite network graph is a typical way of representing these centrality measures in a network. See the exhibit "Kite Network."

Kite Network

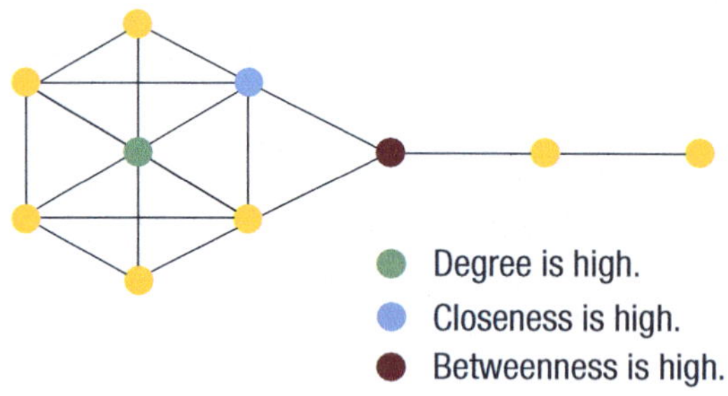

[DA12063]

Network Classification

Nearest neighbor and data mining algorithms, such as logistic regression, can also be used to analyze social networks.

Egonet

A network composed of an ego and the nodes directly connected to it.

A node's nearest neighbors are simply the nodes closest to it in the network. A node and all its nearest neighbors are referred to as an **egonet**, with the center node representing the ego. Insurers and risk managers can analyze customers using an egonet. For example, if the center of an egonet is an employee who has had frequent on-the-job accidents, the co-workers he or she interacts with most may also be accident prone because of either the type of work being performed or personality.

Bigraphs are also useful in network analysis. A bigraph is a network that has two types of nodes. Returning to the previous example, a bigraph could include nodes representing workers and nodes representing their supervisors. This can provide a more complete picture of a network.

Using this type of analysis in social networks makes certain assumptions—that things that are linked are similar. The tendency of people to connect to others who are similar to them is called homophily. When analyzing new customers, insurance and risk management professionals can make predictions about a customer based on his or her closeness to others in a social network.

If a social network is being analyzed to make a prediction regarding the probability of nonrenewal or renewal of auto insurance policies, logistic regression can be used. Two types of attributes are taken into account in this modeling context: **local variables**—traditional modeling attributes that relate to the node (instance)—and **network variables**, which consider the node's interactions within the network.[9] Continuing the renewal example, a local variable would be a customer's age, while a network variable would be how many of the customer's contacts or friends did not renew and instead moved to other auto insurers.

Local variable

In a social network analysis, an attribute that relates to the characteristics of a specific node.

Network variable

In a social network analysis, an attribute that relates to the node's connections within the network.

In a modeling context, each node can be viewed as an instance, described by its local and network variables. This format allows the data gleaned from social network analysis to be used in various data mining algorithms, such as clustering, classification, and logistic regression. See the exhibit "Local and Network Variables Example: Auto Insurance Renewal."

Apply Your Knowledge

Rachel is an interior designer, and her brother, Brian, is a claims professional for Tannery Insurance. On LinkedIn, Rachel is connected to many employees of Tannery Insurance, whom she has met through her brother. Rachel often comments, reposts, or likes homeowners insurance articles posted by employees of Tannery on LinkedIn. Rachel is also connected to many of her own past and current clients. These clients see Tannery's articles on their LinkedIn newsfeeds because of their connections to Rachel. This example illustrates Rachel's high degree of which one of the following?

a. Degree

b. Closeness

c. Betweenness

d. Nearest neighbors

Feedback: c. This example illustrates Rachel's high degree of betweenness, as she is a connection between otherwise separated nodes in this network. This example does not provide the information necessary to determine with whom Rachel communicates the most and is most closely connected to, nor does it provide enough information to determine whom she is most similar to (and who is therefore her nearest neighbor). The number of Rachel's LinkedIn connections is also unknown, although she may very well have many.

Local and Network Variables Example: Auto Insurance Renewal

	Local Variable	Local Variable	Local Variable	Network Variable	Network Variable	Target Variable
	Name	Age	Length of Time With Insurer	Connections With Contacts Who Left Insurer	Strength of Connections With Contacts Who Left Insurer (Scale of 1 to 10)	Policy Not Renewed
Instance	Bennett	28	3 years	8	8	Yes
Instance	Christian	37	7 years	3	9	No
Instance	Tiana	25	5 years	11	6	Yes
Instance	Lucy	55	20 years	7	3	No
Instance	Ralph	30	10 years	15	10	Yes

[DA12064]

NEURAL NETWORKS

Neural networks are on the frontier of data science. They are designed to replicate the functions of the human brain. Although neural networks cannot actually behave like a human brain, they can operate in similar ways when sorting through input data. They can also complete activities that the human brain cannot, such as rapidly performing thousands of mathematical calculations on large amounts of data.

One of the most important characteristics of neural networks is their ability to analyze very large quantities of data. Another is their ability to work with incomplete data. Their analyses can include conclusions based on observations, detected correlations, and new concepts. In the future, neural networks will likely be an important technique for helping insurers and other organizations understand data and develop innovative solutions. Therefore, it is important for insurance and risk management professionals to have a basic understanding of what neural networks are and how they can be applied.

Neural networks are often considered to be a type of machine learning. However, the most advanced neural networks, such as Google's DeepMind, are at the frontier of machine learning and are likely to develop that frontier into a new evolution of data science and big data.

Predictive analytics

Statistical and analytical techniques used to develop models that predict future events or behaviors.

Machine learning begins with a model that has been developed and tested by data scientists to perform **predictive analytics**. As the computer applies the model, it learns from the results and new data.

For example, an insurer has a model to price personal auto insurance based on individual characteristics, such as age, driving experience, and daily distance traveled. If the model is given data about loss results, it may slightly adjust the weight it assigns to daily distance traveled compared with other variables. The computer uses the rules of the original model to produce its predictions.

Neural networks are less dependent on rules than other forms of machine learning. They are able to make independent observations about the data they receive and then provide intuitive results. For example, a neural network may observe a driver characteristic from loss information that had not previously been considered as a rating factor.

Insurers are currently using neural networks for various purposes, including pricing, reserving, and predicting claims. There are studies underway that evaluate the potential for neural networks to assist in developing business strategies.

Mechanics of Neural Networks

Neural networks consist of three layers. The input layer provides data for the network to analyze, the output layer provides results of the analysis, and the **hidden layer** resides between these two layers. The hidden layer acquired its name because the processes used by the computer are not transparent or easily understood. See the exhibit "Diagram of a Neural Network."

Hidden layer
A layer in a neural network in which neurons learn and recode information received from input data.

The input layer consists of nodes that contain data. For example, if an insurer wants to predict the probability that a claim is fraudulent, the nodes in the input layer will contain data about the claim that are possible fraud indicators. A neural network can only work with numerical values. Therefore, any nonnumeral value must be converted to a number. The input nodes in this example may include the length of time the customer has been with the insured, the amount claimed, the date of the loss, the date of report, and the number of individuals involved in the alleged accident. The hidden layer provides links to the input nodes that assign weights to the data. The network multiplies the values of the link weights by the values of the nodes to produce an output value.

In reality, a neural network is more complex than the example above. The hidden layer actually performs various mathematical functions to match inputs to outputs. These functions may employ cluster analysis, **classification analysis**, or linear functions. As the neural network performs these mathematical functions, it develops rules to make predictions. Each time a new set of data is input, the network refines the rules to provide more accurate results. Typically, a neural network uses thousands of **neurons** and links to perform calculations, enabling it to process large volumes of data.

Classification analysis
A supervised learning technique to segment data according to the values of known attributes to determine the value of a categorical target variable.

Neuron
The mathematical function in a neural network that receives input.

Applications of Neural Networks

Neural networks currently have several applications in insurance and risk management, and additional uses are likely in the future as the technology evolves.

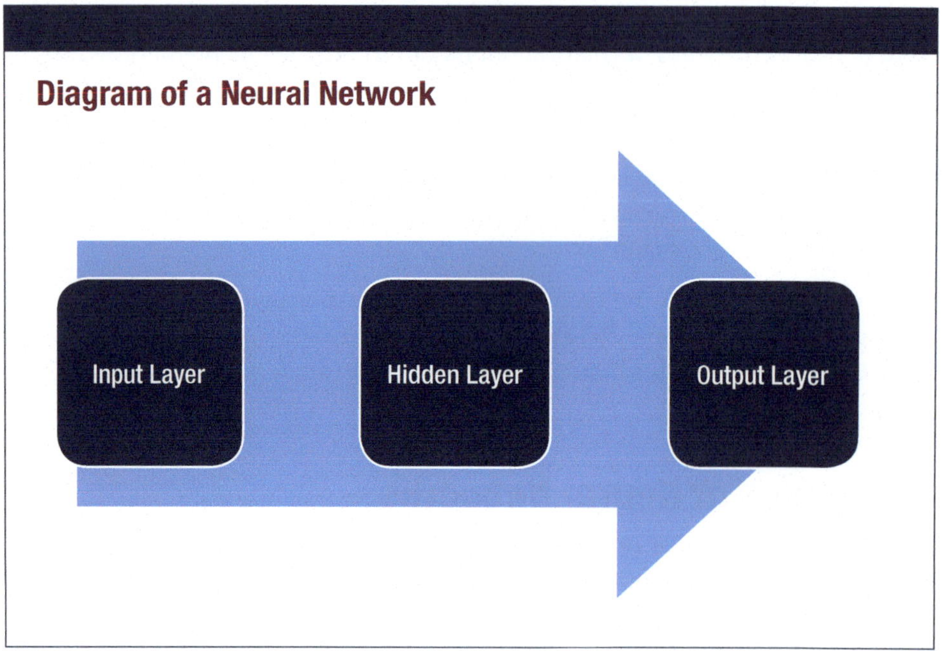

[DA12045]

Neural networks have been used to predict customer retention after premium increases. A clustering technique is applied to customer data according to demographic information. Then a neural network analyzes the clusters to determine the probability of renewal according to changes in the premium.[10]

A study comparing different data science techniques for auto insurance rate-making, including classification trees, linear regression, and neural networks, found that well-developed neural-network models produced more accurate rates tailored to the individual customer.[11]

Working with data that is many times incomplete, neural networks can be used to predict claims durations in long-tailed lines of insurance, such as workers compensation or general liability. It is often important to predict claims duration for several reasons. Longer-duration claims are usually associated with higher severity. Also, open claims require reserves, which tie up an insurer's capital. Additionally, claims with long durations have the potential for adverse development.

Neural networks are more sensitive to nuances than other types of models and are also able to make observations. Therefore, neural networks may provide more accurate and complete information about claims duration.[12]

Further, neural networks can be used in risk management to compare the risks of proposed and current projects to historical results. Data regarding successful and failed past projects is used as inputs to the neural network. Then data regarding the proposed project can be input for the network to predict the probability of success.

Additionally, data regarding an ongoing project can be analyzed by the neural network, predicting the probability of success at each stage. However, the factors that caused previous projects to succeed or fail must be understood to determine inputs for the neural network. It is possible to use a modeling technique, such as cluster analysis, along with human evaluation, to determine those factors.[13]

As demonstrated in the risk management example, neural networks have the ability to interpret big data and provide risk evaluations for insurers or other organizational enterprises. Data scientists can use other techniques, such as clustering, with neural networks to produce more accurate results. These techniques are already being used to predict the solvency, or insolvency, of some financial institutions. It is likely that neural networks will evolve rapidly and develop the ability to recommend strategy.

However, neural networks as they currently exist have some drawbacks. The hidden layer is often too opaque to data scientists, and the methodology and results cannot be properly evaluated. The optimization of the hidden layer(s) must be precisely determined. Optimization is achieved when the prediction at the output layer is evaluated according to actual values. The network must be able to learn from the errors, such as modifying the weights it assigns to different neurons in the hidden layer. However, as with all predictive modeling techniques, there is a risk of overfitting.

Because of the opaque nature of the hidden layer, it may be more difficult for data scientists to determine the cause of the overfitting and correct it if the model does not correct itself. Data scientists and computer engineers are working to resolve these issues, after which neural networks will likely be more widely used in risk management and insurance.

SUMMARY

To use the abundance of text available in a modeling context, the text must first be retrieved, prepared, and structured. Insurers can use claims notes, social media, and news stories to better understand their business and to predict future customers' behaviors. Both traditional and newer modeling techniques can be applied to the results of text mining.

Insurers and risk managers can achieve a better understanding of their customers by studying social networks. They also can use the data provided by social networks, particularly social media networks, to supplement existing customer information and develop more accurate predictive models.

In neural networks, which are capable of handling big data, the data goes into an input layer. The network analyzes that data in the hidden layer, which is where learning occurs. After this analysis, results appear in an output layer. Neural networks are highly complex, and they have the ability to operate in ways similar to the human brain. They are currently used in insurance and risk management for predicting customer retention, underwriting, ratemaking, determining claims durations, and evaluating the risk of new enterprise projects. However, data scientists and engineers continue to work on making the hidden layer more transparent and on optimizing analyses.

ASSIGNMENT NOTES

1. Foster Provost and Tom Fawcett, *Data Science for Business* (Sebastopol, Calif.: O'Reilly Media, Inc., 2013), p. 253.
2. Louise Francis and Matt Flynn, Text Mining Handbook, Casualty Actuarial Society E-Forum, Spring 2010, p. 8, www.casact.org/pubs/forum/10spforum/Francis_Flynn.pdf (accessed May 20, 2016).
3. Provost and Fawcett, p. 257.
4. Sergei Ananyan and Michael Kiselev, "Automated Analysis of Unstructured Texts: Technology and Implementation," www.megaputer.com/site/down/textanalyst_whitepaper.pdf (accessed June 1, 2016).
5. Sholom M. Weiss, Nitin Indurkhya, and Tong Zhang, *Fundamentals of Predictive Text Mining* (London: Springer-Verlag, 2015), p. 70.
6. Robert A. Hanneman and Mark Riddle, "Introduction to Social Network Methods," University of California, Riverside, 2005, http://faculty.ucr.edu/~hanneman/nettext/C5_%20Matrices.html (accessed June 21, 2016).
7. Hanneman and Riddle, "Introduction to Social Network Methods."
8. Bart Baesens, Analytics in a Big Data World (Hoboken, N.J.: John Wiley & Sons, Inc.), 2014, p. 121.
9. Baesens, pp. 126-7.
10. "Neural Networks for Automobile Insurance Pricing," What-When-How, http://what-when-how.com/information-science-and-technology/neural-networks-for-automobile-insurance-pricing-information-science/ (accessed June 3, 2016).
11. Charles Dugas, Yeshua Bengio, Nicolas Chapados, Pascal Vincent, Germaine Denancort, and Christian Fournier, "Statistical Learning Algorithms Applied to Automobile Insurance Ratemaking," Casualty Actuarial Society, August 11, 2003, https://www.casact.org/pubs/forum/03wforum/03wf179.pdf (accessed June 3, 2016).
12. David B. Speights, Joel B. Brodsky, and Darya L. Chudova, "Using Neural Networks to Predict Claim Duration in the Presence of Right Censoring and Covariates," Casualty Actuarial Society, www.casact.org/pubs/forum/99wforum/wf99255.pdf (accessed June 3, 2016).
13. Salvatore Alesseandro Sarcia, Giovanni Cantone, and Victor R. Basili, "A Statistical Neural Network Framework for Risk Management Process," University of Maryland, www.cs.umd.edu/~basili/publications/proceedings/P120.pdf (accessed June 3, 2016).

Direct Your Learning

5

Technology and Smart Products

Educational Objectives

After learning the content of this assignment, you should be able to:

- Determine how artificial intelligence, wireless sensor networks, and computer vision can support underwriting, claims, and risk management.
- Demonstrate how smart products can be applied to risk management.

Outline

Technology and Smart Products

5

EMERGING TECHNOLOGY FOR UNDERWRITING, CLAIMS, AND RISK MANAGEMENT

As emerging technologies move from the fringe to the mainstream, they are increasingly able to liberate decision making from its traditional limitations. Underwriting, claims, and risk management, in particular, have been fundamentally changed by technology's ability to rapidly gather and process massive amounts of previously inaccessible data and to convert it into actionable intelligence.

Imagine the relationship between emerging technologies and decision making as part of a connected ecosystem. See the exhibit "Emerging Technology Ecosystem for Decision Making."

Emerging Technology Ecosystem for Decision Making

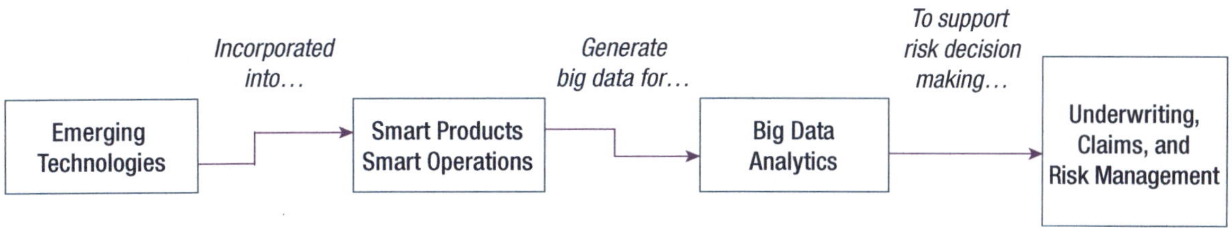

[DA12703]

Relationships among the various components are straightforward. Emerging technologies are incorporated into **smart products**. These products are able to sense their environment, process data, and communicate with other smart products, which are programmed to act and communicate independently. These products and operations generate big data. Applying algorithms to big data generates information underlying smart operations. This process has transformed the management of property, supply chains, transportation, catastrophe response, and workplace safety into dynamic processes that use the accumulation and analysis of real-time data to constantly refine the ability to anticipate and mitigate risk. See the exhibit "Preventive Analytics."

Smart product
An innovative item that uses sensors; wireless sensor networks; and data collection, transmission, and analysis to further enable the item to be faster, more useful, or otherwise improved.

Preventive Analytics

Smart products empower the preventive analytics that lie at the heart of smart operations. As an example of preventive analytics, consider an insurer's sending a text alert to its commercial auto policyholders when a hail storm is approaching and encouraging businesses to move vulnerable vehicles in their fleets to a covered area. A business that follows this guidance will effectively manage its risk by avoiding hail-related damage to its autos and injury to its drivers. Each auto hail claim that is prevented saves the insurer large sums of money, in turn saving its customers money in premium cost. The way in which weather can be accurately predicted for a specific location relies, in part, on sensors located on satellites and deployed as part of a fleet management program.

Preventive analytics leverages modern technology, big data, and advanced analytics to identify root causes and their interactions. It is particularly effective because it can continuously monitor activity—whether arising from humans or machines. By learning patterns, a machine can identify situations or behaviors that are unexpected or will likely produce an unexpected result. Therefore, preventive analytics is forward looking. Consider how computer-vision technology in an auto identifies and analyzes risks, which can then lead to preventive actions. For example, a truck's brakes may automatically be applied because a front-facing camera determines that a vehicle has stopped directly in front of the truck.

Preventive analytics are also able to take advantage of the sheer volume of data available. For example, in the case of fraud prevention, every financial transaction provides data, which a machine can learn and ultimately use to identify both legitimate and potentially fraudulent transactions.

[DA12704]

Artificial intelligence (AI)
The ability of machines to simulate human intelligence.

Wireless sensor network (WSN)
A wireless network consisting of individual sensors placed at various locations to exchange data.

Computer vision
A technology that simulates human vision.

The emerging technologies that form the spine of this ecosystem include **artificial intelligence (AI)**, **wireless sensor networks (WSNs)**, and **computer vision**.

Artificial Intelligence

AI is essentially a computerized simulation of the human brain's ability to form inferences, judgments, and accurate assessments of situations. It empowers automation of tasks that require critical thinking, animating the new generation of smart products, including these:

- Wearables such as helmets that monitor fatigue or wristwatches that measure vital signs can sense, monitor, report, and analyze workers' health or well-being and their surrounding environments. Underwriting data generated by wearables may be specific to one employee or aggregated for a project, team, or organization.

- Drones can be used to gather underwriting and claims data about property damage or different geographic areas. Data generated by drones relies heavily on AI to mine it and form conclusions about detected objects.
- Robots can measure, respond, and produce data for monitored hazards or changing environmental conditions. Sensors in conjunction with high-definition cameras can scan and inspect, for example, bridges for erosion or other unsafe conditions.

Wireless Sensor Networks

Just as AI transforms mere machines into dynamic risk assessment and management tools, WSNs connect individual sensors in ways that simulate a human brain's ability to sense and react to the body's environment. Sensors assess risk by detecting and measuring objects or conditions on a continuous basis; this provides early warning of impending problems or malfunctions and determines whether expected results have occurred. When **smart sensors** also accurately respond by triggering remedial actions, they control risk and help reduce losses and potential claims by appropriately and promptly addressing the situation.

Smart sensor
A specialized sensor programmed to respond in a specific way when a threshold of detection or measurement is reached.

When facilitated through a WSN, sensors become more integrated with the targets they sense. And because the network is wireless, the sensors can be almost anywhere: underwater, airborne, in space, or on rocky terrain. For example, different sensors or wearables may provide health, safety, location, movement, or many other types of data on workers as well as characteristics of the monitored environment. The large amount of raw data collected and transmitted is then analyzed to produce information that makes it more specifically applicable to the project or its solution.

Algorithms are used to analyze the sensor data and relay critical information ("The worker's wrist monitor showed a lowered heart rate and alerted him to stop and take a break") or route critical communications to a manager, emergency response personnel, and other remote workers on site ("The worker's location sensor in his nametag and other sensors in his boots reveal that a fall just occurred at a specific location, with reduced brain activity from his smart helmet, identifying a head injury"). The result is a quicker response, with faster transport and treatment, and ultimately a healthier worker in a safer workplace.

Computer Vision

Computer vision involves the detection, extraction, and analysis of an image or a series of images to develop a deeper understanding of the images. It performs the analysis by developing and using algorithms that can automatically provide visual understanding. While originally undertaken to mimic the human eye in making calculated, reason-based decisions based on the image, computer vision has not managed to fully duplicate these actions, but it has mastered some of them. In some cases, computer vision has the advantage of recognizing specific conditions or symptoms—such as fatigue, which can dull a person's ability to judge, discern, and decide.

Although not a perfect science, computer vision is being used in retail operations for automated checkout lanes; in medical imaging; in automotive safety, particularly in the field of automated vehicles; in surveillance; and in traffic control. And soon, insurers will be able to harness this technology to fortify their ability to review and resolve claims, with computerized recognition of, for example, a photograph of auto damage and an integrated algorithm that estimates the associated dollar value. As opposed to a single human with one pair of eyes, many different cameras (stationary or video) looking at one fixed point or panning a certain area can provide a more comprehensive and integrated view over time. This technology is a blend of data science, engineering, statistics, and algorithms. It has become more specialized, accurate, and reliable over time as related computer technologies have also advanced.

One of the early tenets of computer vision was segmentation, or how the images are seen and mapped. When combined with deep learning, this mapping of features through an algorithm relates to a commensurate action. Computer vision has been used in this way with self-driving vehicles for both risk assessment and risk control. The many cameras and angles from which images are continuously received are matched with actions to recognize or assess risks (such as a car drifting into another driver's lane) and actions to control or mitigate the risk (by, for example, applying the brake or easing into another lane, whichever is more appropriate in the situation).

Computer vision and artificial intelligence can be used in facial recognition software. Cameras capture images of faces, which are matched with file photos or information from other databases. The software then segments the person's face so that it can be easily compared with others. It can even assess emotions from facial expressions. This technology has potential uses in identifying criminals in a crowd or quickly and accurately confirming identities of people boarding an aircraft or entering a secure area.

HOW SMART PRODUCTS APPLY TO RISK MANAGEMENT

Historically, risk managers' assessments of the probability of adverse events were limited by the boundaries of human perception. Today, however, previously imperceptible risk factors, such as a worker's hydration level, the presence of a hazardous chemical in the air, or the catastrophic intersection of seemingly disconnected financial transactions, can be factored into risk management decision making.

This new world of risk assessment data has been revealed by smart products that sense their environment, process data, and communicate with other smart products and smart operations. These interactions generate big data—to which advanced analytics can be applied, ultimately reducing the uncertainty associated with predicting future events.

As technology evolves, the availability and sophistication of smart products that can help refine risk management techniques continue to grow. Here are just a few examples:

- Wearables such as helmets that monitor fatigue or wristwatches that measure vital signs can sense, monitor, report, and analyze workers' health or well-being and their surrounding environments. Data generated by wearables may be specific to one employee or aggregated for a project, team, or organization.
- Drones can be used in surveillance and aerial photography; being unmanned and highly versatile makes them ideal for assessing conditions or risks in dangerous or unknown areas. The data generated by drones relies heavily on other technologies, such as computer vision, image recognition, and artificial intelligence, to mine the data collected and form conclusions about detected objects.
- In addition to performing activities and capturing information from sensors in a workplace, robots can measure, respond to, and produce data for monitored hazards or changing environmental conditions. For example, sensors in conjunction with high-definition cameras can scan and inspect bridges for erosion or other unsafe conditions.

Smart products have introduced a new dimension of depth and precision to risk assessment and control in a variety of contexts, including these:

- Property management
- Supply chain management
- Transportation management
- Catastrophe management
- Workplace safety management
- Construction and engineering management

Property Management

Property managers can use wireless sensor networks (WSNs) to detect and respond to leaks and malfunctions or prevent on-site falls and injuries. For example, temperature and water sensors can monitor heat irregularities and detect the first signs of leakage before tenants (especially lower-level ones in multistory buildings) sustain water damage to drywall, carpets, furniture, or other belongings. Temperature sensors provide alerts before a pipe freezes and are particularly useful in vacant or temporarily unoccupied buildings. Light sensors monitor illumination and provide lighting when needed around the perimeter of buildings, in parking lots, on stairs, and in underground parking garages, eliminating hazards that could lead to liability claims and lawsuits. Motion sensors and surveillance cameras can deter crime before it occurs and document suspicious activities. Thermal sensors, current sensors, and smoke detectors assess impending fire conditions so that first responders can be notified before a fire begins or actions can be taken to lessen the extent and cost of damage if one does occur.

Because the sensors in a WSN work together, multiple buildings can be remotely managed, producing data that shows real-time and historical maintenance reports and service records, as well as comparisons among properties or units, floors, or departments within a property. Some sensors only need to be placed in the desired locations and activated. Many applications allow further monitoring or interaction opportunities. And surveillance cameras, enabled with computer vision, capture images that can be analyzed for additional insights, allowing for loss prevention and reduction and ensuring continuous climate control, controlled power consumption, and compliance with building codes.

Supply Chain Management

Supply chain management involves the risk of not only product, service, or shipment disruptions caused by unforeseen events but also the downstream effects that interruptions cause to other products, services, or shipments. Risk assessment, which involves identifying potential or actual disruptions, and risk control, which involves preventing or reducing disruptions, use many emerging technologies to manage supply chain risks.

For example, radio frequency identification (RFID), which uses radio frequency to identify objects, wireless protocols, and the Global Positioning System (GPS), is particularly important to managing supply chain risks. Supply chain assets were previously tracked using standard bar codes, which must be in close proximity to a reader. In contrast, RFID tags identify assets and compile their characteristics without human intervention.

RFID technology is wireless, supports an automated process, does not require the reader to be in close proximity to the asset, and provides specific information on each asset to facilitate logistics and transport. This technology, especially when used with GPS for additional location tracking, enables a mixed shipment of freight to be identified and tracked without the need to remove any external wrapping. Furthermore, each item of freight can be easily cataloged by the reader according to description and condition, manufacture and expiration dates, arrival location and time, and relationship to current inventory. When a shipment is incomplete or damaged, RFID technology can be used to assess the risk, automatically call for replacements, and manage the replacement process.

Additionally, RFID tags provide unique identifiers, which offer real-time, accurate record storage and retrieval in a closed-loop system. With this readily available, detailed data on supply chain assets, companies can immediately identify discrepancies and interruptions and quickly prevent and reduce supply chain risk. Furthermore, RFID's process-automation capability can generate real-time alerts for those who need to receive the information and oversee remediation.

Other kinds of sensors can empower more precise supply chain management. For example, sensor data can inform a supply chain manager that weather conditions have interrupted the production of parts or that cargo has been stolen.

Transportation Management

Transportation management that facilitates risk assessment and control involves incorporating technologies from the **Internet of Things (IoT)** to connect vehicles and their drivers with solutions for awareness, safety, efficiency, and reliability. These same technologies also help organizations manage their vehicle fleets.

Internet of Things (IoT)
A network of objects that transmit data to and from each other without human interaction.

Some of these technologies even provide driver assistance. Examples include crash avoidance; self-parking; cameras on the back of trucks to facilitate lane changing; and, in some cases, full autonomous driving capabilities enabled by cameras that use computer vision to discern people from other objects or vehicles, as well as to recognize changes in pavement types or abrupt lane changes in construction zones.

Smart transportation is also key to transportation management. As with many smart operations in a variety of contexts, it can be described as a series of layers:

Smart transportation
The integration of strategic vehicle management solutions with innovative technologies.

- A sensing layer, which uses a variety of sensors, cameras, and data-collection capabilities to make (or help the driver to make) necessary corrections and provide information to others
- A communications layer that provides data transmission to and from drivers and managers using wireless protocols that ensure necessary capabilities, such as recording, data uploading, navigating, video recording, and centralized monitoring for both the sensing layer and the service layer
- A service layer, which employs applications using data processing, cloud computing, and storage and analysis of large amounts of the data captured by vehicle sensors and provided by drivers

The results of this interaction among layers are improved remote diagnostics, prompt driver response from real-time analysis of his or her driving habits or physical condition, fuel and/or vehicle repair savings because of implemented corrections, preventive maintenance alerts before a costly mechanical breakdown, and customizable products and services (such as comparisons of nearby hotels and restaurants) to make rides easier for drivers and more enjoyable for passengers.

These advancements are also attributable to the photos, images, diagnostics, trip logs, and other vast amounts of data and statistics created by the sensing layer, analyzed by the service layer, and supported by the communications layer. The resulting data is, in turn, used to monitor performance and further refine the processes.

Telematics

The use of technological devices to transmit data via wireless communication and GPS tracking.

For example, accelerometers, devices that measure acceleration, motion, and tilt, are combined with special software to detect and measure linear motion. Through **telematics**, accelerometer technology can generate information about vehicle fleets, such as operator acceleration and braking. It can also be used for many other applications, such as to detect excessive vibration in an industrial machine that is about to explode and may injure workers and/or damage property.

Additionally, augmented reality technology can integrate a digital experience into a user's physical environment. One such example, head-up displays in or near aircraft and car windshields, reduces distractions for pilots and drivers by displaying information, such as speed and warning signals, within their lines of sight.

Catastrophe Management

Sensors and WSNs are also used in catastrophe management. As long as a sensor can withstand a harsh environment, it can continuously monitor an area for light, temperature, specific gases, and more. Alternatively, a sensor or WSN can measure local changes when a catastrophe is predicted or has occurred.

By continuously sensing the environment, sensors and WSNs can detect and analyze changes over time and help predict a catastrophe and allow for adequate preparation. For example, an accelerometer can continuously monitor earth movements to determine where an earthquake will occur, and underwater pressure sensors can measure water weight on sensors to help determine how fast and in which direction a tsunami will travel. In fire-prone areas, gas sensors, thermal sensors, and anemometers can be strategically placed on the outer proximity of an area to warn of approaching forest fires.

Lidar

A sensor similar to radar that uses infrared light to detect nearby objects.

Lidar is a technology used to, among other things, improve the performance and accuracy of autonomous vehicles. It can work with optical sensors, such as high-definition cameras, to detect images, even through shadows or blinding sunshine. Lidar has applications to catastrophe management, both before and after a natural disaster:

- It provides images even under lighting conditions that are inadequate because of cloudiness, intense sunshine, or shadows. Furthermore, its high-definition three-dimensional mapping technology provides more realistic and usable data than two-dimensional mapping.
- It can capture and produce accurate elevation data, enhancing the mapping of flood-prone areas before a flood and helping to determine the flood

levels that will be reached based on current water levels in surrounding rivers. It can also help identify regions, neighborhoods, or even individual structures that may need to be evacuated before a flood.

- Furthermore, lidar images after a flood, and the additional data it collects on air pressure, temperature, wind turbulence, and location, provide information that assists in prioritizing rescue and remediation efforts. This information can also be used to analyze and compare various flood events.
- Lidar can help determine the optimal location for emergency communications equipment after a disaster disrupts cell or internet service. Models produced using lidar images identify the optimal locations for placing mobile Wi-Fi terminals (linked to satellites) to provide a signal for up to a thirty-mile radius. After a catastrophe such as a tsunami or an earthquake, lidar can provide street-by-street or even structure-by-structure analysis of locations with the highest risk, thus helping rescue and remediation resources be deployed efficiently.

Workplace Safety Management

Many smart products ultimately may be used to improve workplace safety and productivity:

- Wearables allow workers to wear sensors in comfortable and familiar ways (such as in safety vests or work boots) and still have their hands free to do their jobs.
- Drones provide information and help assess and control risks by going into unknown and potentially dangerous areas without putting humans at risk; they can accomplish this on the ground, in the air, or underwater.
- Robots—no longer clunky, human-like machines—operate in close proximity to workers but do more of the repetitive and heavy-lifting jobs. This allows workers to better use their skills and for humans and machines to be better integrated in the workplace.

Construction and Engineering Management

Mechanical sensors detect and measure a physical quantity and produce a signal that is readable by the user or another device. They are generally used with machinery and have many applications in construction and engineering:

- Motion sensors have many applications, including surveillance and security.
- Pressure sensors are similar to strain sensors, which convert pressure or tension into a measurement of electrical resistance.
- Current sensors are useful in protecting electronic systems and batteries from heat buildup.
- Position sensors are used when components are to be activated only when they are in the optimal places for a particular process to continue.

They are used, for example, in car-wash machinery that senses the size of vehicles and adapts the cleaning process accordingly.

- Proximity sensors, slightly different from position sensors, respond when an object reaches a threshold area within range of the sensor. For example, proximity sensors in smartphones can sense the presence of an ear and turn off the backlight and touch-screen functions to save power.
- An inertial measurement unit (IMU) tracks an object's position using accelerometers and gyroscopes. IMUs are used in navigation systems, as orientation (location) sensors in personal devices, and to measure motion in fitness trackers and gaming systems. They are also key sensors for autonomous vehicles.

SUMMARY

Underwriting, claims, and risk management have been fundamentally changed by technology's ability to rapidly gather and process massive amounts of previously inaccessible data and to transform it into actionable intelligence. The emerging technologies at the heart of this revolution include artificial intelligence, wireless sensor networks, and computer vision.

Smart products can be used to enhance risk assessment and control in a variety of contexts, including these:

- Property management
- Supply chain management
- Transportation management
- Catastrophe management
- Workplace safety management
- Construction and engineering management

Direct Your Learning

6

Underwriting Applications of Big Data Analytics

Educational Objectives

After learning the content of this assignment, you should be able to:

- Explain how insurers can use the information from vehicle telematics to improve automobile policy ratemaking.
- Explain how insurers can use machine learning to improve the loss ratio of a homeowners book of business.
- Explain how an insurer can use data mining to improve the underwriting process for products liability risks.

Outline

Underwriting Applications of Big Data Analytics

6

AUTOMOBILE RATEMAKING USING VEHICLE TELEMATICS

Many people are already using telematics in their vehicles: they might use a global positioning system (GPS) for navigation or a Bluetooth system for hands-free phone calls. However, telematics in vehicles is being used for far more than personal convenience. Underwriters can use information provided by telematics to better understand personal and commercial policyholders and to develop more accurate automobile insurance rates.

Auto insurers seek to set reasonable and adequate rates for their products—rates that customers can afford and that allow the insurers to make a profit. Generally, automobile rates are published on a class basis. That is, similar exposures are grouped, and rates sufficient to cover the group's loss experience are charged to each member of that group. Classification plans help ensure rate equity by grouping insureds with similar loss potential. Actuaries and underwriters use a set of standard attributes (variables) to evaluate personal and commercial auto policyholders. However, when they are able to identify additional attributes that affect or reflect potential frequency and severity of loss, they can use this information to create more refined classification systems that produce more accurately priced accounts. The use of telematics presents such an opportunity: new attributes that correlate with auto losses are identified, and auto insurance classes and rates are refined. See the exhibit "Vehicle Telematics."

Vehicle Telematics

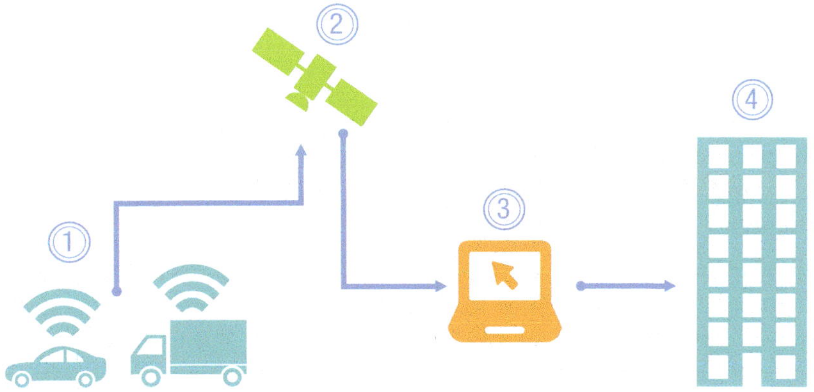

[DA12087]

Traditional Automobile Rating Attributes

Primary rating factors, the major attributes that most states and insurers use for determining the cost of personal auto insurance, include these:

- Territory—Determined by where the auto is normally used and garaged (parked overnight), territory is usually defined by the location of the insured's residence. Rural territories often have lower rates than urban territories because loss frequency and claims expenses tend to be higher in cities. Road conditions, state safety laws, and the extent of traffic regulation are territorial factors that affect the frequency and severity of auto accidents.
- Use of the auto—Insurers normally classify each insured auto for its principal use. Typical "use" categories include driving for pleasure, to work or school, for business use, and for farm use. Rates are generally lowest for farm use and highest for business use, reflecting typical accident statistics.
- Age—Young drivers have less driving experience and tend to be involved in accidents more frequently than older drivers. Therefore, rates for younger drivers are often higher than those for more experienced drivers.
- Gender—In the past, women have tended to have fewer accidents than men in the same age categories, particularly among youthful drivers, so rates are often lower for women than for men. However, this tendency has been changing in tandem with women's driving habits.
- Marital status—Young married men tend to have fewer accidents than young unmarried men, and rates often reflect this tendency. However, changing societal norms are affecting the usefulness of marital status as an underwriting consideration.

Additional attributes that insurers may use for rating include driving record, driver education, years of driving experience, credit score, and other factors that give insight into a driver's general behavior and the auto's use.

Private passenger vehicles owned or operated by a business have very similar underwriting considerations. However, commercial trucks, tractors, and trailers are classified and rated based on these factors:

- Vehicle weight and type—The damage resulting from an auto accident is related to the size, weight, and speed of the vehicles involved. Commercial tractor-trailer rigs can weigh 80,000 pounds or more when loaded, and they often travel at or above the maximum posted speed; hence, these vehicles are more likely than others to cause severe damage when an accident occurs. Large trucks are also difficult to maneuver in heavy traffic or on small inner-city streets, a factor that increases loss potential.
- Vehicle use—Commercial vehicles vary significantly in their amount of road exposure and in how they are used. Some vehicles may be used almost continually to haul goods, while others may be used only to travel to and from job sites, remaining parked most of the time.

- Radius of operation—Radius of operation is another measure of road exposure. The distance traveled, as well as the nature of that travel, can affect accident frequency. Trucks operated over long distances may be more likely to have more severe accidents than those operated locally. There are two reasons for this. First, a driver who operates a truck over long distances may not be as familiar with the route and its hazards as drivers who operate trucks locally. Second, long-distance trucking is likely to be more strictly scheduled. If drivers are rushing to meet a delivery deadline, the potential resulting fatigue and excessive speeds can increase accident frequency.
- Special industry classifications—Special industry classifications include food delivery, waste disposal, farmers, and so forth. From an underwriting perspective, trucks, trailers, or tractors with special industry classifications can present additional concerns and require an underwriter to gather more information.

Vehicle Telematics

There are a few ways to collect vehicle telematics data: through the temporary or permanent installation of tracking devices, through embedded telematics equipment, and through smartphone applications. Telematics devices track driving habits regarding braking, acceleration, speed, cornering, lane shifting, left turns versus right turns, and the time of day the vehicle is driven. The devices then transmit that information wirelessly to a computer.

Telematics can be used simply at a risk-management level. For example, commercial organizations may implement telematics as part of fleet safety programs, as monitoring employees' driving behaviors can lead to safer driving and reduce vehicle accidents. However, the use of telematics for **usage-based insurance (UBI)** is increasing.

Usage-based insurance
A type of auto insurance in which the premium is based on the policyholder's driving behavior.

With UBI, pricing for coverage is partially determined based on driving behaviors. Therefore, an excellent driver who has coverage with UBI will most likely receive a lower premium than he or she would without it. Some of the attributes that telematics accounts for, such as mileage and drive duration, have historically been factored into auto policy rates. However, in the past, the accuracy of that information relied on the customers' perception and honesty. Telematics offers an insurer the opportunity to know, for example, how many miles a policyholder drives at night. But it takes sophisticated modeling techniques to make that information relevant and to determine how much the information should affect rates.

Insurers are not the only ones to benefit from telematics. In addition to benefiting from the potential for lower premiums, customers may enjoy increased safety through driving behaviors that improve based on feedback received.

Vehicle telematics can function as ongoing driver education for those who participate, and society in general benefits from better drivers on the road. For example, parents could obtain data reports illustrating their teenagers' driving behaviors, potentially leading the teenagers to drive better because they know they are being monitored. One disadvantage is that most people who agree to participate in such an endeavor are likely already safe drivers and are simply hoping to obtain lower premiums. This could prevent data drawn from telematics devices from being generally predictive about the driving population as a whole.

Another challenge related to using telematics involves the need to evaluate the data in context. For example, a driver in a congested area will brake harder and more frequently than a driver in a rural area. Although the reason for more frequent braking should be accounted for, the risk of driving in a congested area, rather than on a rural road, must also be evaluated.

Telematics' Effect on Ratemaking

Insurers often divide auto insurance applicants into homogeneous classes, or rating categories, such as "preferred," "standard," and "nonstandard," that reflect different levels of loss exposure. For example, applicants with good driving records and rating factors that suggest they present minimal loss exposure are categorized as preferred. By offering lower rates to this category of insureds, insurers hope to attract and retain good customers. Conversely, applicants with poor driving records or rating factors that suggest they present greater loss exposure are categorized as nonstandard and are charged higher rates. Using telematics allows insurers to better segment drivers into rating classifications.

After a vehicle is monitored through telematics for a certain period of time, an insurer can present the insured with a new rate that takes the driving experience into account. This does not mean that the primary factors for auto rates are ignored, but rather that the telematics information helps provide the insured with a more precise rate.

As a simplified example, assume that a personal auto insurer is attempting to classify a group of customers who have voluntarily signed up for UBI. Without the use of telematics data, the drivers fall into two classes: standard risk and preferred risk. (No customers falling into the nonstandard risk class signed up for UBI.)

Using the attributes provided by telematics, the insurer reclasses the drivers based on a personalized driving score. A score of 1 to 33 represents a nonstandard risk, a score of 34 to 67 represents a standard risk, and a score of 68 to 100 represents a preferred risk.

Loss ratio

A ratio that measures losses and loss adjustment expenses against earned premiums and that reflects the percentage of premiums being consumed by losses.

The insurer finds that by using the telematics' attributes, it is not only able to more accurately class the drivers, but that after twelve months, its **loss ratios** have improved. This is because the insurer can determine that some drivers who were receiving a preferred rate were actually only standard drivers. These standard drivers received tips for improving their driving, and the insurer was able to more accurately predict their losses. Conversely, some drivers who were classified as standard were actually excellent drivers who should have been receiving a preferred rate. By offering these customers a lower rate, the insurer is able to retain their business. Overall, the insurer's loss ratio decreases and its retention ratio increases. See the exhibit "Telematics' Effect on Driving Class and Personal Auto Loss Ratios."

Telematics' Effect on Driving Class and Personal Auto Loss Ratios

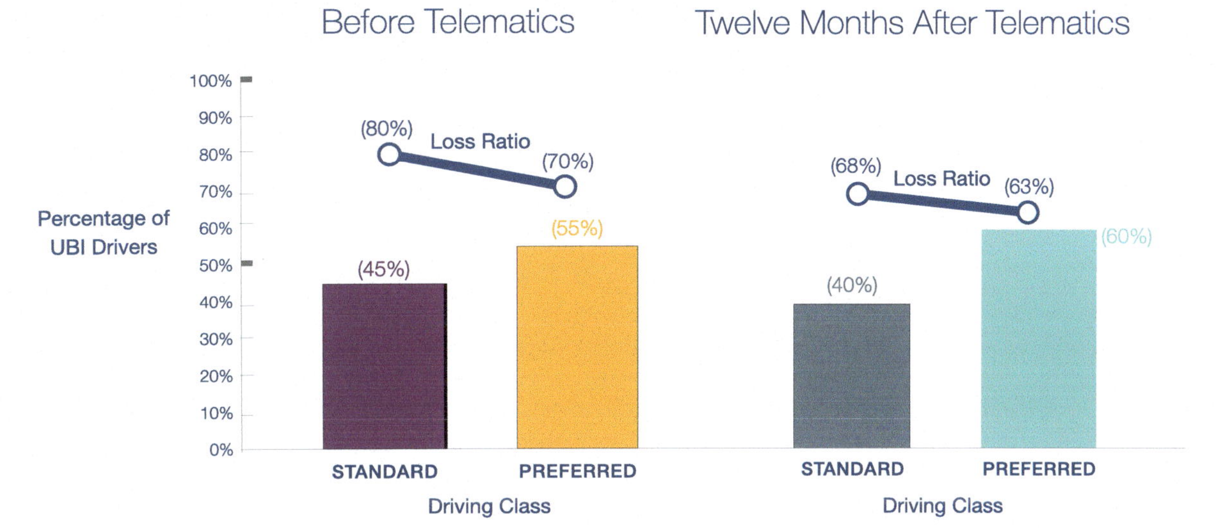

This material is based on Paul Stacy and David Neave, "General Insurance: Telematics," The Actuary, May 8, 2014, www.theactuary.com/features/2014/05/general-insurance-telematics/ (accessed April 4, 2016). [DA12084]

Insurers use loss exposure data generated through telematics to supplement the data they have traditionally used for ratemaking. They analyze this data using sophisticated algorithms, such as generalized linear models, to determine the correlations and interactions among all the rating attributes being considered. This includes traditional rating attributes, such as vehicle use and type, and new attributes generated through telematics, such as braking, acceleration, and time of day. Increasingly, insurers are also using machine learning to aid in the discovery of variable interactions that may not be evident when using a generalized linear model.

For example, an analysis that combines telematics and traditional loss exposure data might show that aggressively accelerating an older auto leads to higher chance of an accident than aggressively accelerating a newer auto. On the surface, this conclusion seems reasonable because older autos might have weaker brakes and other maintenance issues when compared with newer autos. However, this analysis may be distorted by the fact that older autos are owned by a higher proportion of younger drivers than are newer autos.

Younger drivers overall tend to experience more accidents than older drivers. A generalized linear model might need to be supplemented with a machine learning algorithm to analyze all the interactions among these rating attributes. See the exhibit "Privacy and Regulatory Considerations for Vehicle Telematics."

Privacy and Regulatory Considerations for Vehicle Telematics

In the United States, personal auto usage-based insurance (UBI) is voluntary for customers. Because of privacy concerns or poor driving habits, many customers simply do not want their movements to be tracked. Those customers who do opt to use UBI have privacy concerns regarding how their personal information is protected when it is transmitted and who owns the data about a driver's behavior. These concerns are still largely unanswered.

Vehicle telematics data does not typically fall under states' definitions of protected consumer information. There also have not been any substantive legal decisions regarding the data's ownership. Does an insurer have a right to sell telematics data to a third party? Should a court permit telematics data access to prosecutors in criminal cases or to litigants in civil cases? State laws vary regarding this and will no doubt continue to evolve.

Insurers must also ensure that their use of vehicle telematics to make rate changes is transparent and not discriminatory. For example, is it unfairly discriminatory to ask an employee who works second shift to pay a higher premium because modeled data suggests night driving presents a higher risk? Because of such concerns, rating models may be subject to states' rating laws, and insurers should be prepared to explain them.[1]

In comparison, the use of vehicle telematics in commercial organizations is more straightforward. It is an organization's right to monitor its drivers when they are driving company vehicles. The comparative lack of privacy issues is a reason for insurers to devote more resources to developing commercial UBI.

[DA12016]

SEGMENTING HOMEOWNERS POLICIES USING MACHINE LEARNING

Historically, insurers have struggled to make a profit selling homeowners insurance.[2] Before advances in machine learning and predictive analytics, homeowners policy underwriters were limited in their ability to incorporate the many attributes (variables) needed to accurately predict losses. As advances in these fields are made, more data is incorporated into underwriting decisions, and loss ratios improve, thereby enhancing profitability.

Insurers are increasingly finding new correlations between granular data about their customers and loss exposures. Many large property-casualty insurers are using predictive modeling to improve their profits and lower their loss ratios.

To be competitive, small and mid-sized insurers should learn to use machine learning. However, insurers using machine learning must, as with any underwriting classification technique, consider how their decisions will relate to public policy and regulatory concerns and should exercise good judgment at all times.

Need for Rate Adjustment

Assume that there is a small regional insurer with a homeowners portfolio that is struggling to compete with those of national insurers. Additionally, because the insurer is located in the western United States, it is concerned about the increase in wildfires and the corresponding higher claims it has been paying, which are reflected in its loss ratios. The insurer's management does not want to implement a flat rate increase for all its homeowners policies because the significant rate increase it would have to make would drive many of its best customers to other, larger insurers. However, management sees no other way to improve profitability.

Classification analysis supported by machine learning will enable the insurer to simultaneously analyze a large number of attributes (variables) relevant to homeowners loss ratios, as well as the frequency and severity of losses. Often, machine learning reveals relationships and trends not found through traditional ratemaking analysis, which uses complex linear models to model the data relationships. The insurer decides to use machine learning techniques to analyze the components of its loss ratio, improve underwriting guidelines, and more closely match the insurer's premium charges to its loss exposures.

Identifying Loss Ratio Segments With Machine Learning

To develop the sophisticated model needed to refine its homeowners classifications, the insurer must choose the criteria it will use to segment its homeowners policies. It uses traditional rating variables as the attributes to describe each covered home, such as year built, construction type, and location. To be successful, the classification process must also consider the attributes that enable finer distinctions among risk groupings, such as the age of a home's electrical system. While a large national insurer has access to millions of possible combinations of risk classifications, a smaller insurer may assume that it cannot use advanced modeling techniques because it does not have access to a similarly large amount of data. However, its producers' and claims representatives' files may contain more data than it realizes. Even with limited data, machine learning can discover patterns and relationships that will greatly benefit an insurer.[3] See the exhibit "Machine Learning Applied to Homeowners Policy Attributes."

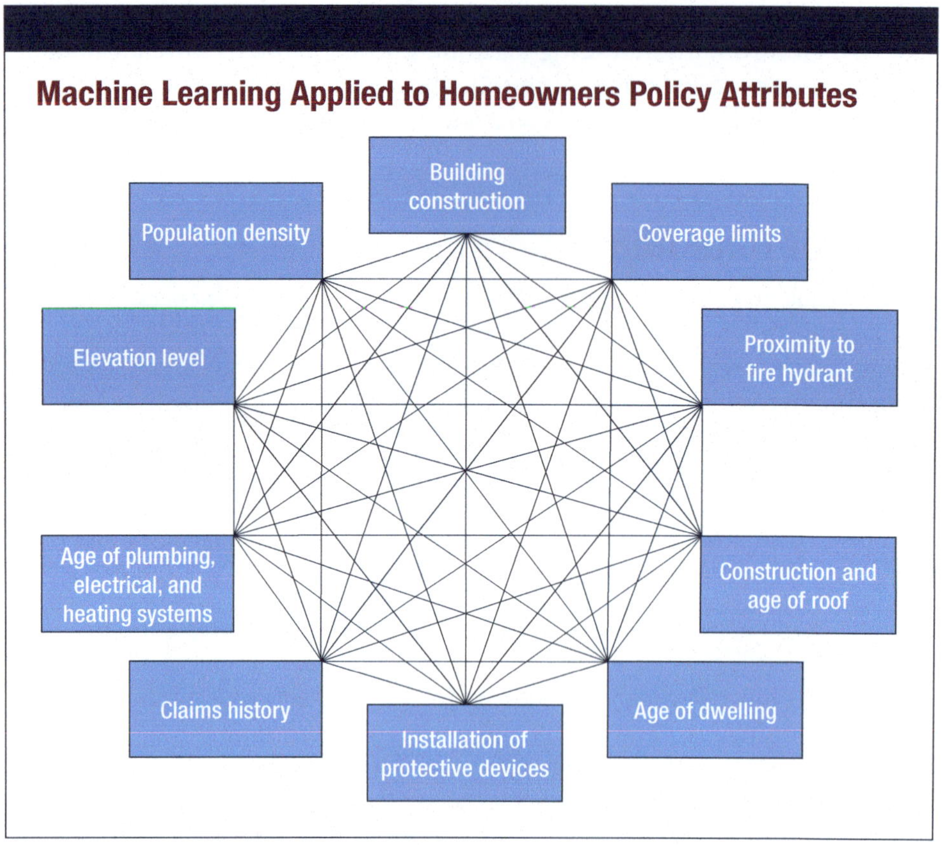

[DA12027]

The insurer also knows that data about underbrush, relative wind speeds, distance between the home and fuel, and other location-specific information could help it better understand the increasing wildfire-related claims and appropriately reflect this loss exposure in its homeowners pricing. The insurer obtains data about the region from a governmental wildfire agency. When that data is introduced, machine learning will be able to discover relationships among all the attributes, both traditional and new.

Evaluating the Effect of Machine Learning on Homeowners Policies

By using machine learning to segment its policies, the insurer sees the effect of attributes and interactions it had not previously considered in its traditional rating model. The insurer notices that loss ratios are not consistent across the segments discovered by the model. Because these segments are based on the interactions of the traditional and the new variables, the insurer is better able to identify which customers to focus on in the future and how to implement the necessary rate increase while still retaining its preferred customers. Customers with a lower loss ratio—who are therefore more profitable to insure—seek a competitive rate; the challenge for an insurer is to provide this while still charging sufficient premiums for customers with higher loss ratios, who are unlikely to leave. See the exhibit "The Effect of Segmenting Homeowners Policies."

The Effect of Segmenting Homeowners Policies

By making only small rate increases for customers in the lower loss ratio segments, the insurer is able to retain most of their business. The insurer makes greater rate increases for those in higher loss ratio segments, which results in the loss of some of these customers but also provides the insurer with the income needed to deal with those customers' loss exposures. Overall, loss ratios decrease as a result of the segmentation and rate changes. Updates to the insurer's underwriting guidelines, based on these customer segment profiles, will only help further decrease loss ratios in the future.

Segments	1	2	3	4	5	Overall Loss Ratio
Loss ratios	30%	45%	70%	105%	120%	74%
Rate increase	5%	7%	10%	20%	27%	
Retention	95%	92%	87%	81%	75%	
Loss ratios after rate changes	27%	40%	67%	101%	105%	65%

As a comparison, look at what would have happened had the insurer decided to run a 20 percent rate increase for all its homeowners customers—an amount that it assumed would have covered its exposures, including the increased wildfire-related claims. Customers with lower loss ratios would have most likely found less expensive coverage elsewhere, therefore lowering retention. Customers with higher loss ratios, who would have a harder time finding coverage with other insurers, would be more likely to stay, leaving the insurer with the least profitable segment of its customer base. Although the loss ratios in Segments 1, 2, and 3 are lower than they are with machine learning, the disproportionate amount of customers left in the unprofitable segments compared to those left in the profitable segments means that the overall loss ratio for the book of business is not improved.

Segments	1	2	3	4	5	Overall Loss Ratio
Loss ratios	30%	45%	70%	105%	120%	74%
Rate increase	20%	20%	20%	20%	20%	
Retention	50%	62%	75%	81%	85%	
Loss ratios after rate changes	22%	35%	63%	101%	108%	74%

[DA09632]

Without machine learning, finding the segment with the characteristics that best match each policy would be extremely time consuming. When a computer performs the task, the specificity of the attributes defining the segments reduces the need for subjective judgments and facilitates more automated underwriting. For example, the model may discover that a segment of homes that are less than 1,500 square feet, have new or updated heating systems, and are at an elevation of less than 2,000 feet has lower loss ratios. Without machine learning, the insurer probably would not have found this correlation. Going forward, the insurer can target this segment of customers using an underwriting scoring model, which allows producers to offer this segment of customers a desirable rate (provided that they meet other criteria). As new attributes become relevant—such as changes to home construction or new building codes in the region—the computer can be trained to account for them.

The insurer has managed to achieve its goal: it has increased rates, lowered overall loss ratios, and become more competitive in the market place. By increasing rates only slightly for those customers whose homes fall into the segments with low loss ratios, the insurer retains those customers and will likely attract similar customers to whom it can offer this competitive rate. By raising premiums for those customers whose homes indicate greater loss potential, the insurer helps cover its rising claims costs. And those insureds may then become motivated to implement personal risk management techniques and make upgrades to their homes in an effort to lower their premiums. For example, the insurer could offer an incentive for insureds who replace their wooden roof shingles with noncombustible materials or replace single-pane windows with dual-pane windows. See the exhibit "The Connected Home."

The Connected Home

More and more people are purchasing systems that enable them to remotely monitor and adjust their homes' heating and cooling and security systems. What opportunities do these devices offer insurers? Personal lines insurers are investigating ways to incorporate smart home devices into homeowners insurance policies by offering discounts to policyholders who install a water sensor or smoke detector that sends alerts to the insured (or even a plumber or the fire department).

Personal lines insurers may even develop usage-based homeowners insurance, similar to that now offered for auto insurance, in which rates would be partially based on wireless data sent from devices within the home.

[DA12029]

UNDERWRITING PRODUCTS LIABILITY RISKS USING DATA MINING

Any business that makes, sells, distributes, or even gives away products has loss exposures that can lead to products liability losses. This is because retailers, distributors, and manufacturers can become liable when products cause injuries to consumers. Social philosophy favors consumers, and laws that hold businesses liable for their products have increasingly expanded. When underwriters evaluate accounts, they consider products' potential to harm the public.

The most important pieces of information in products liability underwriting are the nature of a product and, more specifically, the product's inherent hazards. For some newly introduced products and emerging technologies, it is difficult to rely solely on traditional underwriting guidelines for information regarding the products' liability loss exposures. Data mining can help underwriters more accurately analyze and price products liability loss exposures.

As an example, assume an insurer specializes in providing general liability coverage, including products and completed operations, for cosmetics manufacturers. For some time, the insurer has been comfortable with its approach to assessing risk and underwriting accounts; however, the underwriting department wishes it had more information with which to price the loss exposures of newly developed products. Recent news reports have highlighted concerns about a cosmetics product currently on the market, including a related lawsuit that involved a large settlement amount.

Fortunately, the manufacturer of this product is not an insured of this insurer. However, based on concerns about the possibility of a similar lawsuit being made against one of its insureds, the insurer would like to invest in predictive modeling to make more informed underwriting and pricing decisions for its current accounts. Unsure of how to discover emerging risk trends and where to start collecting data with which to build a model, the insurer contracts with a team of data scientists to deploy data mining techniques to discern possible considerations that the insurer previously may not have factored into its underwriting guidelines.

Discovering Emerging Risks

The team of data scientists determines two approaches it will use to discover emerging risks in the cosmetics liability insurance customer segment. First, the team will apply cluster analysis, an unsupervised learning technique, to find out whether there are any patterns in the recent large claims. Supervised learning and predictive modeling require known attributes and a known target variable—for example, if the insurer wants to predict liability claims based on the presence of red dye. In contrast, cluster analysis allows for a broader view of the data being examined so that relationships the insurer did not previously consider become apparent.

Second, working with a vendor that gathers social media data, the data scientists will use text mining to search social media for references to the products manufactured by the insurer's customers. Text mining of social media can help underwriters determine the inherent hazards of a product because consumers' reactions to products can be monitored before liability claims are filed; however, the use of text mining is not limited to social media. The insurer could also use text mining to search through its claims files. The more details an insurer has about its products liability claims, the more accurately it can price similar exposures.

Cluster Analysis

Cluster analysis is an ideal technique to determine what data has in common. The similarity of two instances (examples) can be measured by the distance between the data points that represent them. A shorter distance indicates a higher degree of similarity. In the current example, the insurer is not sure what its large products liability claims have in common—but a cluster analysis will sort the claims data into groups so the insurer can determine this.

When performing a cluster analysis, data scientists and actuaries often use k-means, which indicates the number of clusters within which the model should group the data. Those experienced with cluster analysis can suggest an appropriate value for "k"; however, the cluster analysis may have to be performed a few times with different numbers of clusters. In the clustering process, each data point (representing, in this case, a claim) is assigned to the cluster with the centroid closest to the data point. The center of each cluster is then recalculated using the data points within the cluster, and the process is repeated until the data points within each cluster and the location of the centroids stay the same, or change minimally. This process is sometimes called nearest neighbor clustering.

The cluster analysis reveals a correlation between long-lasting cosmetics containing a certain ingredient (ingredient X) and products liability claims. See the exhibit "K-Means Cluster Analysis: Cosmetics Ingredient."

Text Mining

One of the insurer's long-standing customers, a large manufacturer of various brands of cosmetics, recently released a new makeup line that contains ingredient X, which the cluster analysis showed is related to a higher incidence of claims. While the products have not been on the market long enough to trigger any claims or to be included in the cluster analysis, the insurer is curious about consumers' responses to the products so far. If their responses have been negative, the insurer will have an additional incentive to review and reunderwrite the account.

The team searches the acquired social media data, which the vendor has prepared for text mining, for the name of the newly released cosmetics line. The intent behind this search is not to determine how many times the product is

K-Means Cluster Analysis: Cosmetics Ingredient

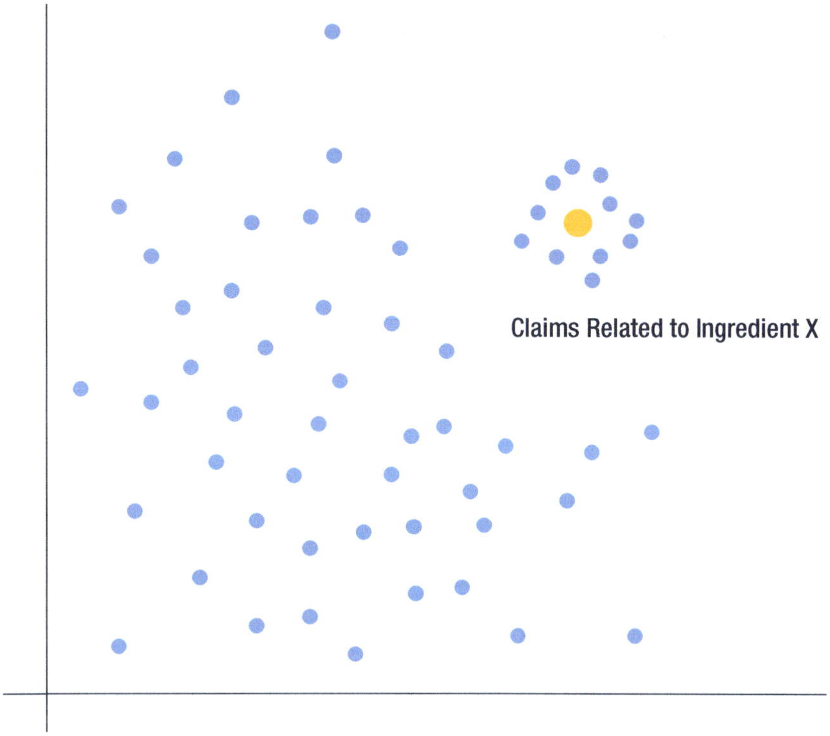

[DA_12013]

mentioned, but rather to determine the sentiment behind mentions of the product.[4] The data scientists equate a positive sentiment with terms, used in conjunction with the product name, such as "improved," "love," and "lasting." They equate a negative sentiment with terms such as "rash," "burning," and "bumpy"—terms that, in this context, relate to an allergic reaction and are more likely to trigger liability claims than terms such as "expensive" or "fades." While the manufacturer itself might be interested in more generic negative reactions, such reactions are not the focus of the insurer's study. See the exhibit "Text Mining Social Media for Sentiment Scores of Cosmetic Products."

Surprisingly, the results of the text mining do not show a significant negative response to the new products containing ingredient X. The team of data scientists wonders whether there is another attribute that, in combination with ingredient X, is influencing the results of the cluster analysis. After re-examining the cluster of claims, an underwriter who is working with the team points out that most of the claims were related to higher-priced products containing ingredient X.

Text Mining Social Media for Sentiment Scores of Cosmetic Products

New Product With Ingredient X	Negative Sentiment Score	Neutral Sentiment Score	Positive Sentiment Score
Foundation	30	50	20
Lipstick	20	60	40
Powder	30	50	20
Total	80	160	80

[DA12015]

An additional cluster analysis confirms that there is a higher incidence of claims related to ingredient X for products for which customers paid over $40. There could be a variety of reasons for this, such as customers having higher expectations for such products or that customers affording such products have more resources with which to file lawsuits. However, the insurer now has the attributes and the target variable with which to build a predictive model.

Predictive Modeling for Emerging Risks

A predictive model would not have been an appropriate tool to use before the cluster analysis because the insurer did not know what relationships it was looking for. Now that the intent of the model is clear, a predictive model can be developed.

This example is simplified in that the insurer is looking for two attributes that lead to product liability claims. In a more realistic and complex scenario, the insurer, working with the data scientists to analyze the data mining and using its insurance professionals' knowledge and past experience with liability claims, could determine which of the products' attributes are important in terms of product liability—for example, ingredients, price, allergic reaction warning label, average consumer age, and so forth—and all these could be included in the predictive model.

The insurer will use its predictive model to review existing accounts and make appropriate underwriting decisions. An account that manufactures a certain percentage of high-end products containing ingredient X may require a rate increase; an account that manufactures only these high-liability products may be considered for nonrenewal.

From a risk management perspective, the insurer can use the valuable information it has gained from data mining to help its customers. For example, the insurer knows that while, generally, a manufacturer is not responsible for rare and unforeseeable allergies and susceptibilities that might exist in a particular person, if a manufacturer knows that a product could adversely affect a large number of people, it has a duty to provide an adequate warning on the product label. The insurer will recommend that any account that manufactures products containing ingredient X, regardless of whether those products are high end, place a warning on the product label. At the very least, this warning and accompanying instructions for use will provide the manufacturer with a defense that could reduce any damages in a products liability lawsuit.

The insurer will also use the predictive model to underwrite new accounts. By more accurately predicting the likelihood of claims, the insurer will be able to determine which accounts it should accept to insure and what pricing levels are required to maintain profitability for the line of business.

SUMMARY

Telematics provides underwriters with additional attributes they can use for more precise classification of drivers and ratemaking. Despite the benefits of telematics, there are still concerns about data privacy and about appropriate use of data gleaned in rate changes. The better that underwriters understand the predictive models they use, such as generalized linear models, the better they will be able to explain telematics' legitimate effect on ratemaking.

Machine learning allows insurers to incorporate more attributes in their underwriting decisions. A fully trained segmentation model can find meaningful patterns in data and automatically segment policies. This allows underwriters to analyze the segmentation and make more-informed rate changes, which improves loss ratios and customer retention.

Data mining can help an insurer properly evaluate an account's products liability loss exposures. Particularly when evaluating products with uncertain risk characteristics, underwriters can benefit from this approach, rather than rely on traditional underwriting guidelines. Cluster analysis can reveal similar products, text mining of social media can find customer reactions to products, and predictive modeling can help to predict claims and, therefore, an account's loss exposures.

ASSIGNMENT NOTES

1. Dimitris Karapiperis and Birny Birnbaum, Aaron Brandenburg, Sandra Castagna, Allen Greenberg, Robin Harbage, and Anne Obersteadt, *Usage-Based Insurance and Vehicle Telematics: Insurance Market and Regulatory Implications*, National Association of Insurance Commissioners and the Center for Insurance Policy and Research, March 2015, p. 58, www.naic.org/documents/cipr_study_150324_usage_based_insurance_and_vehicle_telematics_study_series.pdf (accessed March 31, 2016).
2. Dax Craig, "Driving Profitability in Homeowners Coverage: Examining 'Mitigatable' Losses," Property Casualty 360, July 7, 2014, www.

PropertyCasualty360.com/2014/07/07/Driving-Profitability-in-Homeowners-Coverage-exami (accessed April 12, 2016).

3. Peggy Brinkmann, "Why Big Data Is a Big Deal," Milliman, August 5, 2013, http://US.Milliman.com/Insight/2013/Why-Big-Data-is-a-Big-Deal/ (accessed April 12, 2016).

4. For more information regarding sentiment analysis, see Haruna Isah, Paul Trundle, and Daniel Neagu, "Social Media Analysis for Product Safety Using Text Mining and Sentiment Analysis" (Artificial Intelligence Research Group, University of Bradford, 2014).

Direct Your Learning

7

Claims Applications of Big Data Analytics

Educational Objectives

After learning the content of this assignment, you should be able to:

- Explain how network analysis and clustering can be used to detect claims fraud.
- Explain how classification tree analysis can be used to identify and assign complex claims.
- Explain how business process analytics can be used to improve claims processes.

Outline

Claims Applications of Big Data Analytics

7

DETECTING CLAIMS FRAUD WITH NETWORK ANALYSIS AND CLUSTERING

Insurers have incorporated the expanding field of data analytics into many aspects of their operations, but they've been especially quick to embrace its use in fraud detection. Network analysis, made possible by data analytics, is a particularly useful method of detecting and preventing ever-evolving fraud schemes.

About 10 percent of the property-casualty insurance industry's incurred losses and loss adjustment expenses stem from fraud.[1] Insurers attempt to detect fraud by identifying patterns, controlling underwriting at the points of sale, and using special investigation units (SIUs). Advances in data mining techniques—including network analysis and clustering—are enabling insurers to more effectively identify patterns in fraudulent claims activity. Insurance and risk management professionals therefore benefit from understanding how to analyze links in a social network and clusters of data points.

Suppose that a regional insurer is concerned about its auto-related claims. In particular, this insurer has experienced a significant increase in the number and settlement amounts of auto physical damage claims. While its claims representatives and SIU currently identify 1 percent of its auto claims as fraudulent, the insurer's upper management believes, based on industry data, that the number of fraudulent claims is actually much higher. The insurer is hesitant to spend its resources on increasing its claims staff, nor does it want to continue to raise its auto rates because of the increase in claims. Investing in data mining and predictive modeling seems to be the best long-term solution.

The insurer will conduct these activities to identify fraudulent claims:

- Detect claims fraud through traditional fraud indicators and through mining social media data
- Apply network analysis by examining links and suspicious connections
- Apply cluster analysis to discover claims characteristics that might indicate fraud

Detecting Claims Fraud

The insurer's claims representatives were already following the insurer's protocol for identifying fraudulent claims. Insurers rely on claims representatives to notice indicators of possible claims fraud and to conduct appropriate investigations. Examples of fraud indicators include an insured or a claimant who pushes for a quick settlement or has too much or too little documentation. However, the claims representative must conduct a balanced investigation once fraud is suspected because fraud indicators are not proof of fraud.

Fraud-fighting organizations, such as the National Insurance Crime Bureau, publish lists of claims-fraud indicators. In addition, the insurer has developed its own lists of indicators and uses a computer program to detect characteristics common to fraudulent claims. Such programs analyze vast amounts of data across different lines of insurance to identify claims patterns and other similarities that may indicate fraud. Several organizations, such as Insurance Services Office, Inc., offer electronic antifraud databases that contain claims-related records or provide access to public records that may be used to gather evidence of fraud. Based on which indicators are identified, claims representatives decide whether a case warrants review by the SIU.

Although the insurer is already taking many of the appropriate steps to identify fraudulent claims, some fraud still goes undetected. One reason for this is that the insurer is using fraud indicators, the traditional approach to fraud, which means that it's depending on fraud that has happened in the past. Intelligent and innovative fraudsters will change their approaches and patterns, limiting the usefulness of these indicators.[2] The traditional approach to detecting fraud is also highly subjective and depends on claims representatives' experience in the field. A more automated approach would allow for greater objectivity and enable new claims representatives to be more effective in less time.

The insurer has begun encouraging its claims representatives to search social media for any indicators of fraud, and it will continue to do so. Claims representatives can often find evidence that someone may be lying by comparing his or her social media posts with his or her statements in a claim. For example, a car could be reported as stolen on Thursday while photos show it in the insured's driveway the next day. Or a claimant could complain of extreme back pain but post a status update about dancing.

As useful as these methods may be, however, truly efficient use of data mining and predictive modeling to detect fraud goes a step further and analyzes not only social media posts but connections within a network as well.

Applying Network Analysis

Network analysis can be applied to social media through social network analysis as well as to claims files to detect possible fraud. Certain situations indicate possible fraud, such as multiple people living at the same residence claiming an auto accident in one month or numerous claims involving the same auto repair shops and/or doctors. While a claims representative might be able to pick up on these signs, it would likely be by chance. A particular street address or a doctor's last name would not be included among traditional fraud indicators. By using a machine to analyze the networks, connections are readily detected.

The insurer conducts a network analysis and discovers a fraud ring in which a relatively small number of drivers and auto body shops have participated. The repair shops have been marking up their claims for repair times and parts used to make a profit. All the participants in the fraud ring—the drivers, witnesses, and auto repair shop owners—know each other and are in the same social network. The exhibit shows a simplified diagram of a fraud ring. See the exhibit "Network Analysis of Fraud Ring."

Network Analysis of Fraud Ring

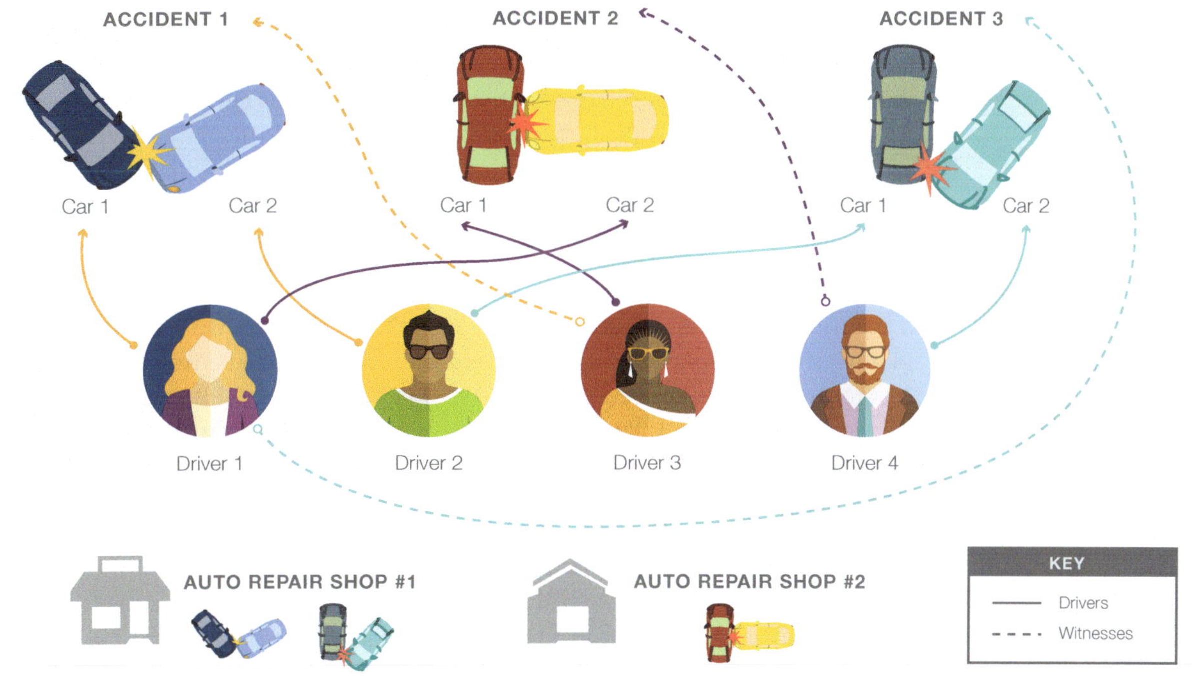

[DA12085]

Applying Cluster Analysis

The insurer wants to train a predictive model to help identify fraudulent claims as they are submitted. It has the attributes it has already used as fraud indicators, and it has identified a fraud ring through the use of network analysis. However, the insurer believes that some fraud has still gone undetected.

One of the limitations in building predictive models is that they are based on historical information—attributes the insurer has already identified as being associated with fraud.[3] This creates several problems. First, because insurers do not identify all fraudulent claims, they often do not have all the historical information needed to develop an effective predictive model. In addition, fraud is ever evolving, with fraudsters constantly changing their tactics and targets, so the predictive model may quickly become outdated. The insurer needs a way to identify new fraud trends as they emerge.

A solution to the problems inherent in predictive models—and an alternative to the already performed network analysis—is unsupervised learning by means of cluster analysis. The cluster analysis will use k-means to group data into clusters of claims closest in distance (and therefore similar) to each group's centroid.

Suppose that the regional insurer performs a cluster analysis on all its auto physical damage claims. The results show a cluster of claims amounts ranging from $8,000 to $10,000. This cluster draws the claims department's attention because it is removed from the other auto physical damage claims clusters, the amounts of which are primarily either under $2,000 or from $3,000 to $4,000. Several of the claims in the outlier cluster are confirmed fraudulent claims. A claims representative confirms that several of the other claims in the cluster were flagged as suspicious. It is highly unlikely that all the claims in the cluster will be found to be fraudulent; most likely, one or more other attributes, in combination with the claims amount, will distinguish the fraudulent claims. Essentially, the fraudulent claims are outliers within the already outlying cluster.

The insurer's SIU now has sufficient reason to investigate this cluster of claims. If a significant number of claims are confirmed to be fraudulent, the insurer has just discovered another attribute (or attributes) it can include in its predictive model. Claims likely to be fraudulent will be referred to an experienced claims representative or the SIU. However, the fraudulent activity identified by this cluster analysis will eventually be suppressed, and fraudsters will develop other schemes to defraud the insurer. The insurer must be prepared to reevaluate the attributes in its predictive model, and it will probably have to perform additional cluster analyses as time goes on. Doing so will allow the insurer to stay ahead of many fraudulent claims instead of relying on dated indicators.

Apply Your Knowledge

Karen is the claims supervisor for the homeowners insurance division of Millstone Insurance. She has instructed all the claims representatives who report to her to examine claimants' social media accounts for any indications of fraud. How could Karen best use information from social media to detect and prevent fraudulent claims?

Feedback: To best use social media data, Karen should work to implement technology that would allow her team to analyze not only social media posts from individual claimants but also connections within a network. Social network connections often reveal fraud rings and other useful information. However, the team must follow the insurer's policies and relevant laws regarding privacy.

USING CLASSIFICATION TREE ANALYSIS IN CLAIMS ASSIGNMENT

A relatively small percentage of claims account for much of the costs to insurers. Some of the high-cost claims can be easily identified at the time of first report, such as the total loss of a building from fire, a major auto accident, or a plant explosion. However, many claims develop gradually into significant losses. For example, someone who at first seems to have only minor injuries in an auto accident may later claim to have a serious back injury. A homeowner may litigate an insurer's decision that flood, not wind, was the cause of a loss. An employee may initially appear to have a minor shoulder strain from lifting boxes, but may later require surgery.

How can a risk manager or insurer identify a claim at the time of first report that is likely to develop into a severe loss?

This discussion will focus on identifying potentially serious workers compensation claims. When an insurer identifies a serious injury, it usually assigns an experienced claims adjuster to handle the claim. It also often assigns a nurse case manager to help manage the medical treatment of the injured worker.

Medical costs represent more than half of workers compensation claims costs, and medical expenses continue to increase. Where permitted by state law, a nurse can direct an employee to an appropriate physician or medical center. This provides a benefit to the injured worker as well as the insurer. A risk manager can identify potential modified-duty work assignments after learning of an employee's temporary or permanent restrictions.

To use these resources effectively, the claims or risk management professional must first identify the claim as serious or potentially serious. Many insurers are using predictive analytics to do this as soon as a claim is reported.[4]

Insurers have large quantities of claims data, and models can be developed based on this data. Risk managers can use their own data, or they can use their insurers' or third parties' data to identify potentially serious claims. For example, because of the increase in opioid use in workers compensation claims, which often results in addiction for the employee and increased costs for the insurer, there is now interest in predictive models to identify injured workers who are likely to have problems with chronic pain and opioids.[5]

Complex claim

A claim that contains one or more characteristics that cause it to cost more than the average claim.

An insurer has been experiencing an increase in its workers compensation loss ratio for several years. An actuarial review of the claims data indicates that there has been an increase in the cost of **complex claims**.

The actuarial review noted that 15 percent of claims reported during the previous five years were of high severity. Of these, only 5 percent were identified as serious at the time of first report. The remaining 10 percent gradually developed into severe claims. Most of the gradually developing claims were initially assigned to a medical-only or inexperienced adjuster. When surgery or litigation occurred, the claim was then transferred to an experienced adjuster; however this did not typically occur for a period of thirty to ninety days after the first report of injury.

The actuarial review team recommended development of a predictive model to identify potentially complex claims within a short time after they are reported. These claims could then be assigned to experienced claims adjusters and other appropriate resources. The insurer's management team agreed with the recommendation, and a data science team was assembled to develop the model.

Overview of the Procedure

The data science team included a claims manager, along with a data scientist and an actuary from the review team. This group began by examining data from the actuarial review to identify characteristics of claims that gradually developed into severe losses.

After identifying these characteristics, the team decided on the type of analytical technique to use to develop a predictive model. Afterward, they tested the model on claims data to evaluate its effectiveness.

Information Gain by Complex Claims Attributes

The data science team looked for attributes that were known within a week of first report in the claims data for gradually developing complex claims. These were the attributes most often present in the complex claims:

- Claim reported more than five days after date of injury.
- Heavy-duty work inherent in job, such as construction, delivery driver, or nursing assistant.
- Employer does not provide light-duty work.
- High school education or less.
- Lower-than-average wages.
- Age greater than fifty.
- Job tenure less than one year.
- Prescription for opioids at first medical visit.
- Physician known to prescribe opioids.

- Complaints of severe pain.
- Previous significant injury claim.
- Comorbidity present, such as obesity or diabetes.
- Attorney representation at time of first report.
- Back injury.
- Knee injury.
- Shoulder injury.

Each attribute was independently analyzed for the information gain it provides in classifying a claim within a week of first report as "complex" or "not complex." The attributes were then ranked according to their relative information gain. See the exhibit "Information Gain From Attributes for Identifying Complex Claims."

Information Gain From Attributes for Identifying Complex Claims

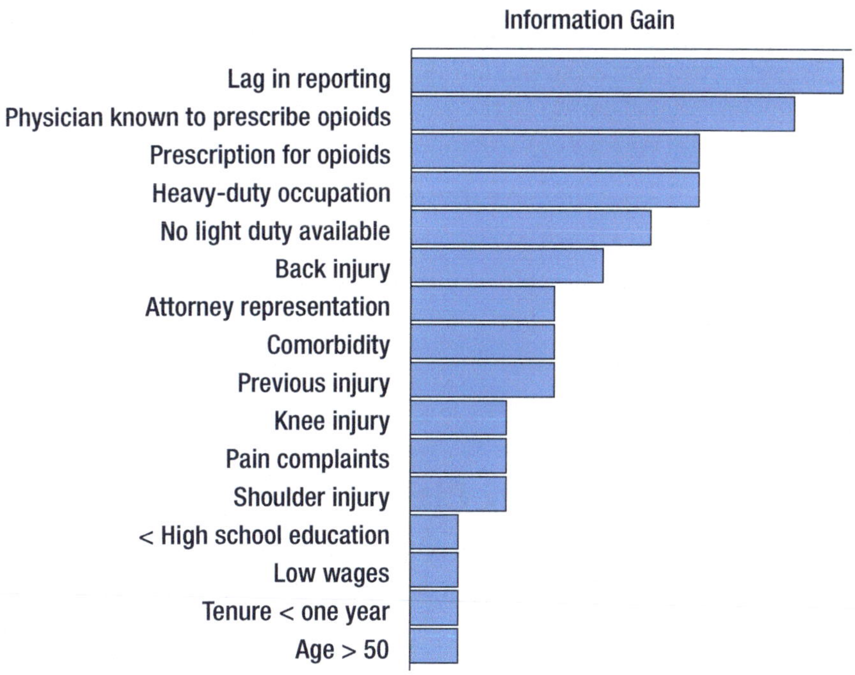

[DA12080]

These are the five attributes that proved most telling regarding whether a claim would develop into a complex claim: reporting more than five days after the date of injury, a physician known to prescribe opioids, a back injury, a heavy-duty occupation, and no light-duty work available at the claimant's employer.

Using a Classification Tree to Illustrate Attributes of Complex Claims

The data science team used a classification tree technique to develop a predictive model based on the attributes of complex claims. With a machine learning algorithm, the computer recursively built a tree by analyzing different splits in the values of attributes in various sequences.

To simplify this discussion, the illustration presents a classification tree showing several of the most important attributes. In reality, the tree would be much more detailed, with many more predictive attributes. See the exhibit "Classification Tree for Predicting Complex Claims."

Note that the sequence of attributes in the tree does not strictly follow the relative information-gain ranking of the attributes. That is usually the case, because the information-gain ranking for the attributes was developed independently of the other attributes. However, the attributes represented by each node in the tree depend on the attributes (and their values) that sit above them.

Combination of nodes
A representation of a data attribute in a classification tree.

Because whether the claim was reported more than five days after the date of injury is determined to be the most informative attribute, it is listed as the root node. Note the **combination of nodes** and branches that lead to a "complex claim" classification at the leaf nodes. This sequence leads to that classification at the bottom of the exhibit:

- Claim reported more than five days after date of injury—Yes
- Treating physician known to provide opioids—No
- Opioids prescribed at first medical treatment—No
- Back, shoulder, or knee injury—Yes
- Heavy-duty occupation—Yes
- Light-duty work available at the employer—No

Validating the Complex Claim Model

The data science team used a portion of the claims data to develop the predictive model. This data was the training data. The target variable is categorical, indicating whether or a not a claim is classified as "complex" or "not complex." Holdout data was used to test the classification tree model to determine its predictive accuracy on data that was not used in its development.

A key measure of the predictive model's effectiveness is lift. Lift is based on a model's accuracy and precision. See the exhibit "Lift From Using a Predictive Model for Complex Claims."

The insurer used 10,000 claims with known outcomes to evaluate the model's lift, of which 3,000, or 30 percent, are complex. The model predicts that 2,000, or 20 percent, of the total claims are complex (positive predictions)

Classification Tree for Predicting Complex Claims

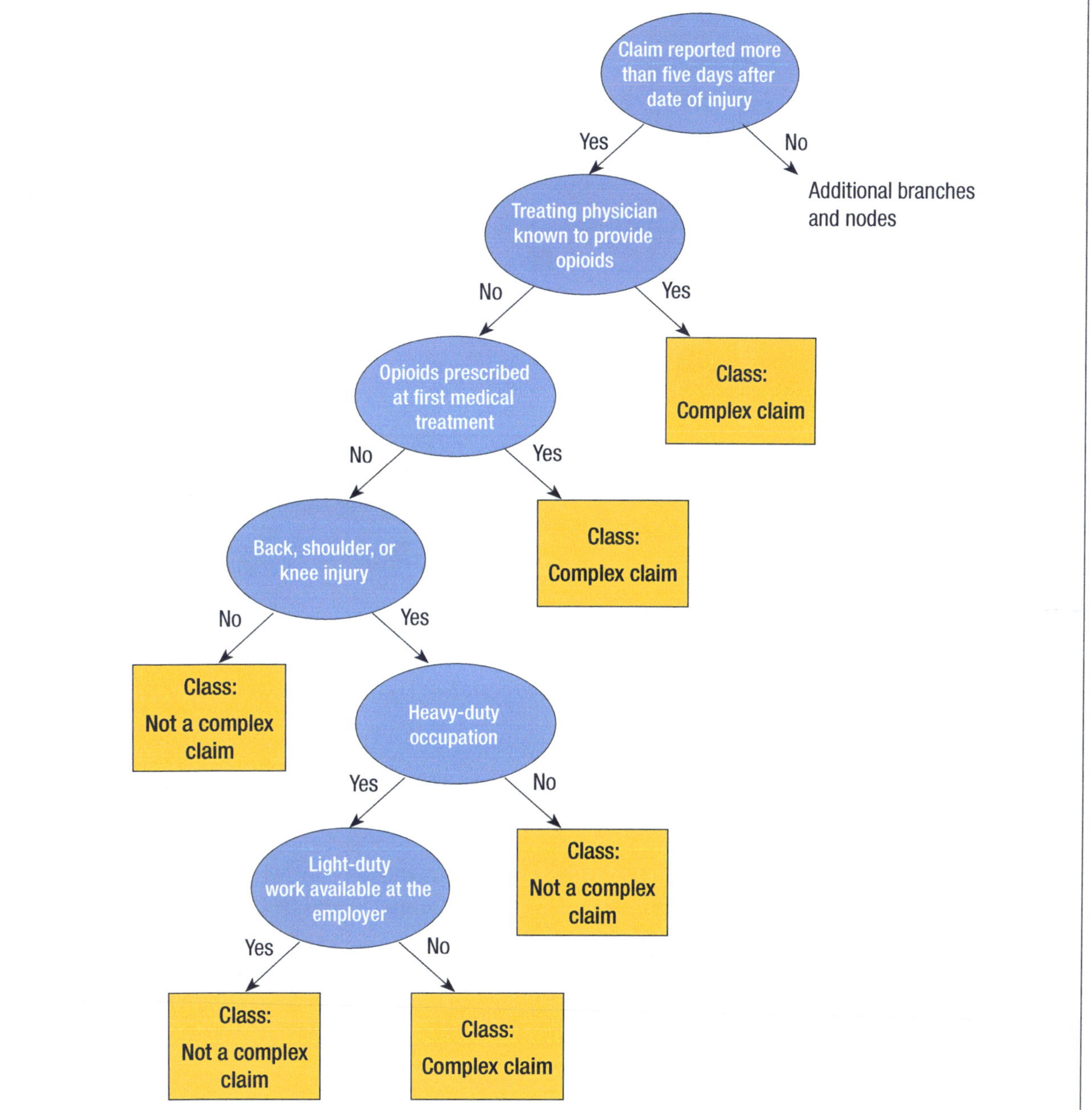

[DA12081]

and the model's precision is 60 percent, meaning that 1,200 of the predicted complex claims are truly complex (true positives) and 800 are not (false positives). Then, the claims are ordered with those predicted as "complex" listed before ones predicted as "not complex."

Lift From Using a Predictive Model for Complex Claims

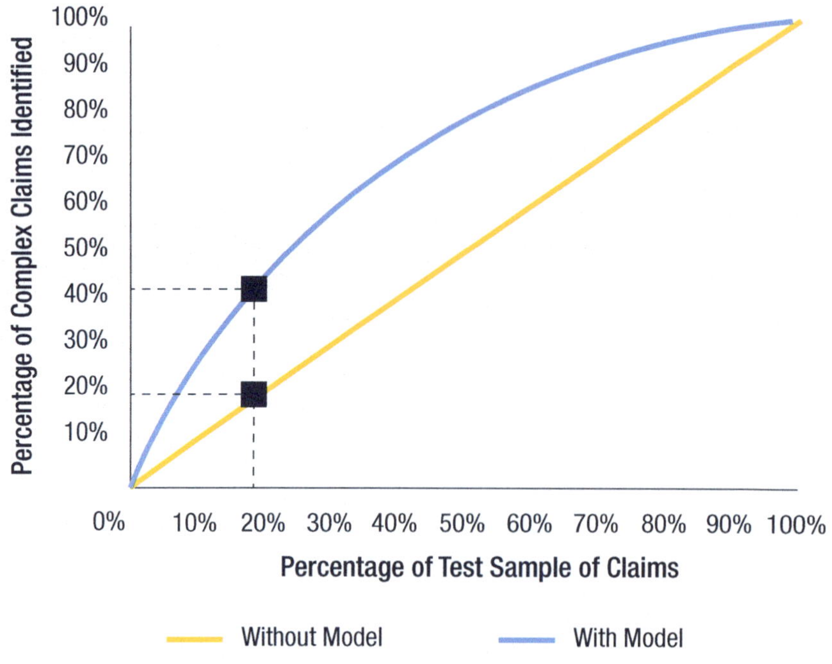

[DA12082]

Assume that the insurer's experienced adjusters have the capacity to handle only an aggregate of 2,000 claims. If the first 2,000 claims in the order specified by the model (therefore, all 2,000 are predicted as "complex") were assigned to experienced adjusters, then, on average, 1,200 (40 percent of the 3,000 complex claims) would actually turn out to be complex. This is a significant improvement over randomly assigning 2,000 claims (20 percent of the total claims) to the experienced adjusters, for which, on average, only 600 (20 percent of the 3,000 complex claims) would be complex. This improvement allows the insurer to more effectively use claims resources. The lift is calculated by dividing the model percentage by the nonmodel percentage. Therefore, 40 percent is divided by 20 percent, resulting in a lift of 2.

Complex Claims Reporting

The insurer's claims reporting procedure begins with a claim reported online or by telephone to its claims intake unit. The intake unit then directs claims to the appropriate office based on the geographical location of the accident. Each office has a claims assignment team that assigns claims based on whether the first report indicates that the injured employee is losing time from work. Catastrophic claims, such as severe burns or head injuries, are assigned to a senior claims adjuster.

The data science team recommended that one office test the predictive model on new claims. Each new claim determined likely to be complex by the model is assigned to an experienced claims adjuster. At the end of a month, the data science team reviews the results to determine the model's effectiveness. Through machine learning, the model adjusts the weights assigned to each of the attributes to better predict complexity.

As claims are better identified as complex at first report, an insurer can more effectively use claims resources. It is not effective or efficient to have inexperienced claims representatives handling claims that have the potential for significant complexity and high cost. Such claims representatives may fail to take appropriate actions to mitigate a claim's severity. Conversely, it is not efficient for experienced claims representatives to handle simple claims that could be effectively managed by less-experienced employees.

Apply Your Knowledge

Describe the steps to develop a model that predicts complex claims.

Feedback: The first step is to determine the attributes of complex claims from training data. Then, the relative importance of each attribute should be ranked. The data science team must decide on the type of data analytics technique to be used. The attributes in the model should be weighted according to their relative importance in predicting claims complexity. After the model is developed, it should be validated by testing it on holdout data.

IMPROVING CLAIMS PROCESSES WITH BUSINESS PROCESS ANALYTICS

Claims activities are critical to an insurer's performance for several reasons. First, many customers have more contact with insurers' claims representatives than with any other employees and form their impression of the insurer based on how their claims are handled. Second, claims are the largest financial obligations of the insurer. Claims representatives are responsible for claim payments and setting case reserves, which have significant effects on an insurer's financial performance. Third, the salaries and expenses of their claims departments represent significant administrative costs for insurers.

Using big data and data analytics can improve claims processes. Insurers have extensive data about their claims, and that data can be analyzed and models developed to increase efficiency and cost-effectiveness. Claims professionals should understand their insurers' overall claims processes and how data analytics can be applied to achieve business goals. Risk managers should also understand the claims processes of their insurers and third-party administrators to evaluate how effectively their claims are managed.

To illustrate how claims processes can be improved using data analytics, this discussion focuses on an insurer that wants to improve its auto claims processing. Improvement objectives include assigning a claim to a representative with the appropriate experience level, ensuring timely contact with the insured, identifying potential fraud and subrogation opportunities, and reducing the time between report of a claim and its conclusion.

Overview of the Procedure

The procedure that the insurer decides to follow to achieve its goals involves these steps:

- Diagram the claims handling process
- Decide how business process analytics can be applied to this process
- Use process mining to develop a map of claims handling procedures
- Apply data analytics to improve the claims handling process

Business Process Analytics and Claims

These are the six major activities in the claims handling process:

- Acknowledging and assigning the claim
- Identifying the policy
- Contacting the insured or the insured's representative
- Investigating and documenting the claim
- Determining the cause of loss, liability, and the loss amount
- Concluding the claim

Various activities are associated with each of these six major categories. Investigating and documenting the claim involves identifying how the loss occurred, witnesses, potential fraud or subrogation opportunities, and other information that may vary with each claim. Determining the cause of loss, liability, and the loss amount is based on facts discovered during the investigation. Concluding the claim may range from payment for minor property damage to a decision in a complex lawsuit. See the exhibit "Activities in the Claim Handling Process."

Business process management (BPM)
A systematic, iterative plan to analyze and improve business processes through life-cycle phases to achieve long-term goals and client satisfaction.

Business process management (BPM) can be applied to the claims handling process to improve customer service, efficiency, and cost-effectiveness. The goal of BPM is to optimize a business process, such as claims handling. To achieve this, BPM begins with exploratory analysis of the current process and then develops models for improvement. Data analysis is used in gathering intelligence as well as developing models.

Activities in the Claim Handling Process

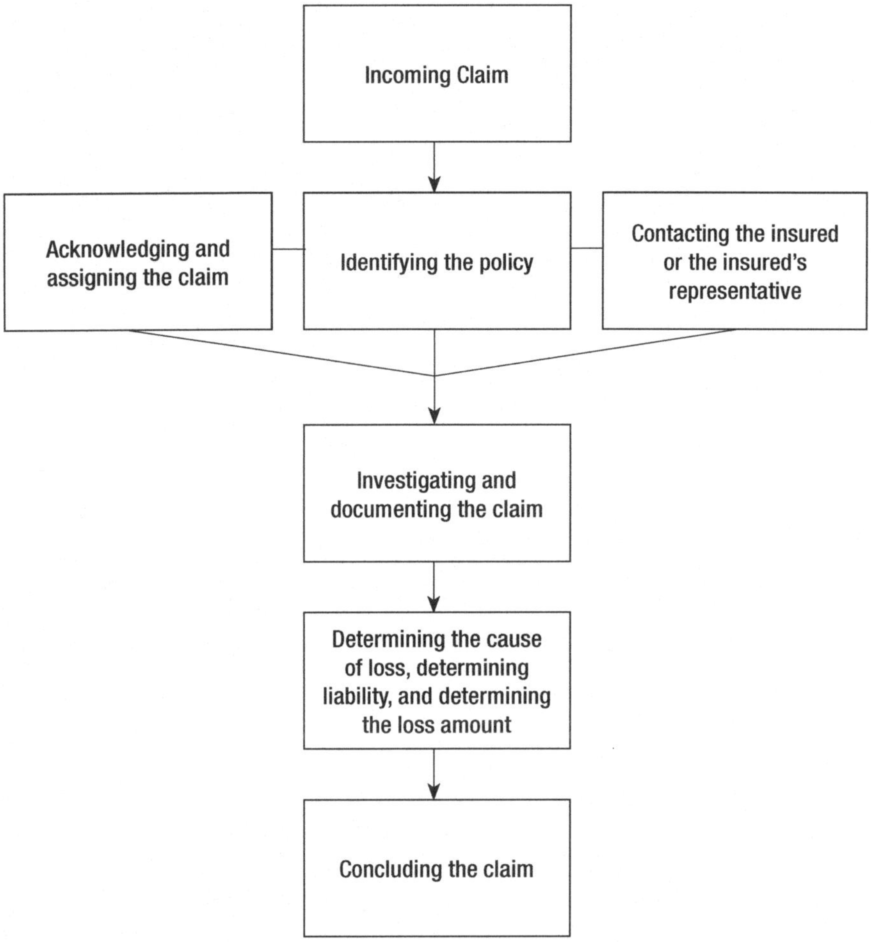

[DA02305_1]

Process Mining Applied to Claims

Process mining uses data analysis techniques to explore data regarding an existing process, such as claims handling, to provide an understanding of the entire process. Process mining differs from typical data mining in its application of results to an entire process rather than one specific area, such as claims costs.

Process mining
The use of exploratory data analysis to provide insights about a business process and identify potential improvements.

Process mining of the claims handling process begins with data analysis of claims activity logs to identify claims handling activities and the timing of them. The first phase in the process mining of the insurer's auto claims involves **process discovery** of claims activities. The activity log for each claim shows the date and time when each activity began and ended. See the exhibit "Example of an Auto Insurance Claim Activity Log."

Process discovery
The use of data analysis to identify the activities involved in a current process.

Example of an Auto Insurance Claim Activity Log

Claim Number	Start Time	Completion Time	Activity
A101	9-12-20XX 08:33	9-12-20XX 08:34	Received claim
A101	9-12-20XX 09:14	9-12-20XX 09:28	Assigned claim
A101	9-13-20XX 10:22	9-13-20XX 10:57	Contacted insured
A101	9-14-20XX 14:17	9-14-20XX 15:02	Reviewed policy
A101	9-15-20XX 11:09	9-27-20XX 11:27	Investigated the claim
A101	10-14-20XX 14:56	10-14-20XX 15:57	Determined the cause of loss, liability, and the expected loss amount
A101	12-15-20XX 08:09	12-17-20XX 08:17	Concluded the claim

[DA12055]

Process map

A diagram of a process that is based on the results of process discovery.

Process instance

A discrete activity in a business process.

An algorithm analyzes all the claims data for the previous year and calculates the duration of each activity. The results of this data analysis are used to create a **process map**, which shows the workflow of the claims handling process and the average time elapsed before each **process instance** is completed. See the exhibit "Claims Handling Process Map."

The process map allows the insurer to understand the average length of time for each process instance in the current claims process and set benchmarks. The average time to assign a claim is five hours on the day of report, which complies with the insurer's best practice of assigning a claim on the same day it is reported. However, the average time it currently takes to contact the insured is two days, which is longer than the insurer's best practice of one day.

The average lengths of time needed to investigate the claim, determine the cause of loss and liability, and conclude the claim are difficult to evaluate. The claims data includes claims with minor property damage that can be settled within a few days as well as claims with serious bodily injury and questionable liability that may take several years to resolve. The average duration of these activities for all types of claims is not helpful in determining how efficiently and effectively the claims are being managed.

The insurer will need to combine process mining with data analysis techniques to gain a better understanding of what is involved in the investigation and resolution of different types of claims. Additionally, the insurer would like to better identify potential fraud and subrogation opportunities and assign claims to representatives with the appropriate experience levels. Another goal is to integrate data analysis throughout the entire claims process to monitor and evaluate how different types of claims are investigated, managed, and concluded.

Claims Handling Process Map

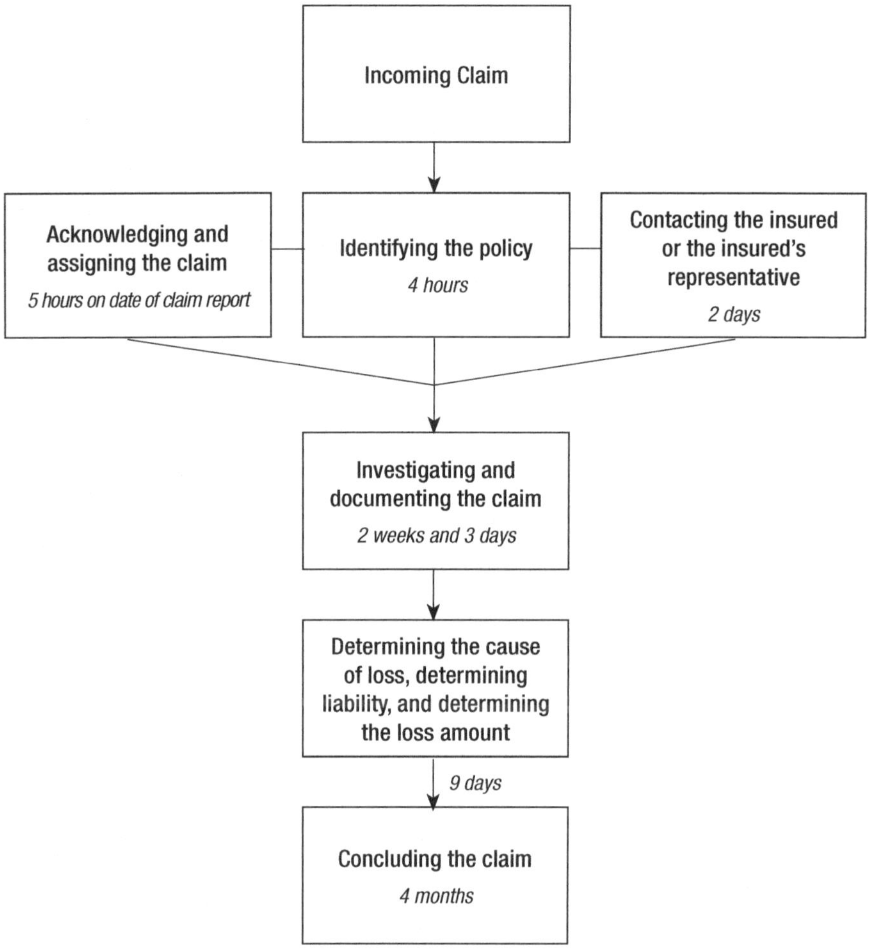

[DA12054]

Improving Claims Processes With Data Analytics

The insurer's data science team must decide on the data analysis techniques that will help the insurer improve the claims handling process throughout the instances in the process map. The team selects the techniques of cluster analysis and classification trees.

Cluster analysis can be used to create clusters of similar claims according to various attributes. These attributes are not known in advance because cluster analysis is an exploratory technique without any predefined variables. Clusters of claims instances would be expected to group around attributes associated with claim severity. For example, a cluster may contain high-cost claims involving bodily injury. Another cluster may contain low-cost claims involving only property damage. After the initial clusters have been created, each one can be further analyzed for additional attributes. For example, a cluster of high-cost claims could produce more clusters according to attributes of litigation or subrogation. However, it is possible that claims instances could cluster around other variables, such as how long claims are open. The same iterative process would be applied no matter how the data is clustered. Cluster analysis would continue to be applied until the data scientist has a good understanding of the relationships between significant variables.

After the cluster analysis is complete, the characteristics of the clusters can be used as attributes to develop classification trees with which to assign new claims according to target variables such as "complex"/"not complex," "fraud"/"no fraud," and "subrogation"/"no subrogation." Logistic regression could then be used to estimate the probability of each of these outcomes to enable the insurer to determine the appropriate resources for each complex claim.

Based on the results of the clustering, classification, and logistic regression analyses, appropriate time frames can be assigned for each claims activity. At designated intervals, such as every six months, managers can review claims data to determine how well individual and aggregate claims are meeting the time frames. Other aspects of claims activities can also be evaluated, such as average settlement amounts, litigation results, fraud investigation outcomes, and subrogation amounts recovered.

Through machine learning, the models will continue to improve in their ability to predict target variables, such as complex claims, fraud, and subrogation.

Apply Your Knowledge

Process mining of the claims process begins with:

a. Diagramming the claims process

b. Data analysis of claims logs

c. Cluster analysis

d. Machine learning

Feedback: b. Process mining of the claims process begins with data analysis of claims logs.

SUMMARY

Data analytics is particularly helpful to insurers in the area of fraud detection and prevention. While many insurers already operate programs that automatically search for traditional fraud indicators, there are opportunities to expand into network analysis and cluster analysis and thereby catch more emerging fraud trends.

If insurers and risk managers can accurately predict complex claims that are likely to develop into high-cost losses, they can assign those claims to experienced claims adjusters and other appropriate resources, such as nurse case managers. Including a claims professional on the data science team can help with selection of the most important attributes. Analysis of known complex claims can provide information to determine the relative importance of each attribute. A classification tree technique works well for this type of model. After the model is developed, it should be validated against a different set of data. Also helpful is testing the model on new data during a trial period to evaluate the model's effectiveness.

Business process management can be used to improve an insurer's claims processes. Process mining is used to develop a process map of current claims activities, referred to as process instances, and the average duration of each process instance. Once the insurer has an understanding of the current process, cluster analysis is used to explore the claims data and to identify various attributes and their relationships. This information is then used to design classification tree models for claims activities, such as claims assignment, fraud investigation, and subrogation potential.

ASSIGNMENT NOTES

1. Insurance Information Institute, "Insurance Fraud," January 2016, www.iii.org/issue-update/insurance-fraud (accessed June 13, 2016).
2. Roosevelt C. Mosely Jr. and Nick Kucera, "The Use of Analytics for Claim Fraud Detection,"http://support.sas.com/resources/papers/proceedings14/1837-2014.pdf, p. 4 (accessed June 14, 2016).
3. Roosevelt C. Mosely Jr. and Nick Kucera, p. 10.
4. "Predictive Modeling Flags Potentially Costly Workers Comp Claims," *Business Insurance*, www.businessinsurance.com/article/99999999/NEWS080105/120809957/predictive-modeling-flags-potentially-costly-workers-comp-claims (accessed June 6, 2016).
5. Denise Johnson, "Travelers' New Predictive Model Targets Chronic Pain, Opioid Use," *Claims Journal*, April 11, 2016, www.claimsjournal.com/news/national/2016/04/11/270032.htm (accessed June 6, 2016).

Direct Your Learning

8

Risk Management Applications of Big Data Analytics

Educational Objectives

After learning the content of this assignment, you should be able to:

- Explain how classification analysis can be used to analyze the data generated from sensors to help prevent employee injuries.
- Explain how text mining and social network analysis can be used to assess reputation risk.
- Explain how clustering and linear modeling can be used for loss development.

Outline

Risk Management Applications of Big Data Analytics

8

PREVENTING EMPLOYEE INJURIES WITH SENSOR DATA

Part science and part art, workplace accident prevention has always relied on data—usually about past accidents—to inform decisions about appropriate risk management techniques. Often, analysis of accident causation focuses on either a single unsafe act or condition. However, even the simplest accidents are the by-product of multiple actions and complex interactions of conditions. Therefore, workplace accidents and their causes are ideal subjects for the application of data analytics techniques.

Traditional methods of workplace accident analysis cannot always account for or even recognize all relevant contributing factors and how they conspire to cause an accident. Data analytics represents an evolutionary step forward in workplace accident prevention in two significant ways:

- It empowers the collection of information from sensors that record thousands of data points about workers and the workplace environment. The most prevalent of these devices are wearable sensors (wearables), which collect data about a worker's biological attributes and physical condition through continuous contact with the worker's body via wristbands, eyeglasses, footwear, helmets, gloves, or other clothing accessories. The law is evolving as to the application of federal and state regulations governing data ownership, health privacy, and security breaches to wearables.
- It creates the potential for the use of predictive models to estimate accident probabilities more precisely than existing methods, most of which are limited by linear decision-making processes that cannot accommodate large amounts of data. Machine learning allows for the rapid, continuous analysis of otherwise imperceptible relationships among myriad variables to improve the accuracy of predictions about accidents and the best ways to stop them.

Traditional Workplace Accident Analysis Techniques

Employee injury prevention efforts have grown in number and complexity as industrialization and technology have spread around the globe. Safe, healthy workers are happier, more productive, and, in the long term, less expensive than the alternative. Prominent categories of traditionally effective workplace accident analysis techniques include these:

System safety

A safety engineering technique also used as an approach to accident causation that considers the mutual effects of the interrelated elements of a system on one another throughout the system's life cycle.

Root cause analysis (RCA)

A systematic procedure that uses the results of the other analysis techniques to identify the predominant cause of the accident.

Failure mode and effects analysis (FMEA)

An analysis that reverses the direction of reasoning in fault tree analysis by starting with causes and branching out to consequences.

Criticality analysis

An analysis that identifies the critical components of a system and ranks the severity of losing each component.

Fault tree analysis (FTA)

An analysis that takes a particular system failure and traces the events leading to the system failure backwards in time.

- **System safety** analysis—System safety analysis examines an organization as a whole to identify potential sources of accidents. System safety relies on a number of specific techniques for identifying and analyzing hazards and for determining how these hazards can lead to system failures and accidents. These techniques can estimate the probability of particular kinds of breakdowns and suggest cost-effective ways to prevent these system failures.
- **Root cause analysis (RCA)**—A root cause is the event or circumstance that directly leads to an accident. Determination of an accident's root cause allows organizations to discern the cause of a harmful event and prevent such an event from recurring by identifying and mitigating the actions, inactions, conditions, or behaviors that caused the harmful event.
- **Failure mode and effects analysis (FMEA)** and **criticality analysis**—FMEA and criticality analysis allow an organization to determine which risks to address and in what priority. Their goal is to prevent or reduce the severity of a harmful event by identifying the order in which critical failures should be addressed. Once the most critical failures have been identified, the team or risk management professional should develop a plan of action and implement it by assigning specific actions (remedies) to specific personnel. The remedies should include eliminating the failure mode, minimizing the severity (consequences), reducing the occurrence, and improving detection.

An organization's safety program may combine elements of these accident analysis techniques. For example, a **fault tree analysis (FTA)**, which incorporates RCA concepts and FMEA techniques, can be used to identify potential accidents and to predict the most likely system failures. FTA identifies various ways of "breaking" the fault tree; that is, it interrupts the sequence of events leading to system failure so that the failure itself can be prevented.

Imagine the risk manager of a multinational construction contractor. With workers engaged in intense labor involving heavy or flammable materials at unsafe heights, building construction is one of the world's most hazardous occupations. Falls, structural collapse (of trenches and scaffolds, for example), electrical shock, improper use of safety equipment, and repetitive motion injuries all represent threats the risk manager must consider in workplace accident analysis.[1]

Fault tree analysis allows the risk manager to examine the series of events and conditions that led to an accident. The accident appears at the top of the fault tree, and the events necessary to produce it appear as branches. This is known as the fault tree's top event.

The tree's branches are connected by "and" gates (shaped like beehives) and "or" gates (shaped like fish tails). These gates represent the causal relationships between events, which are depicted as rectangles within the tree.

For example, the "and" gate directly below the injury found in rectangle A indicates that event A can occur only if all four events in rectangles B, C, D, and E occur first. If any one of those four events does not occur, the accident cannot occur either.

In contrast, an "or" gate signifies that any one of the events leading to the gate is sufficient to cause that event. A fault tree also can be used to calculate the probability of an accident if the probabilities of the causal events are known. See the exhibit "Sample Fault Tree."

Sample Fault Tree

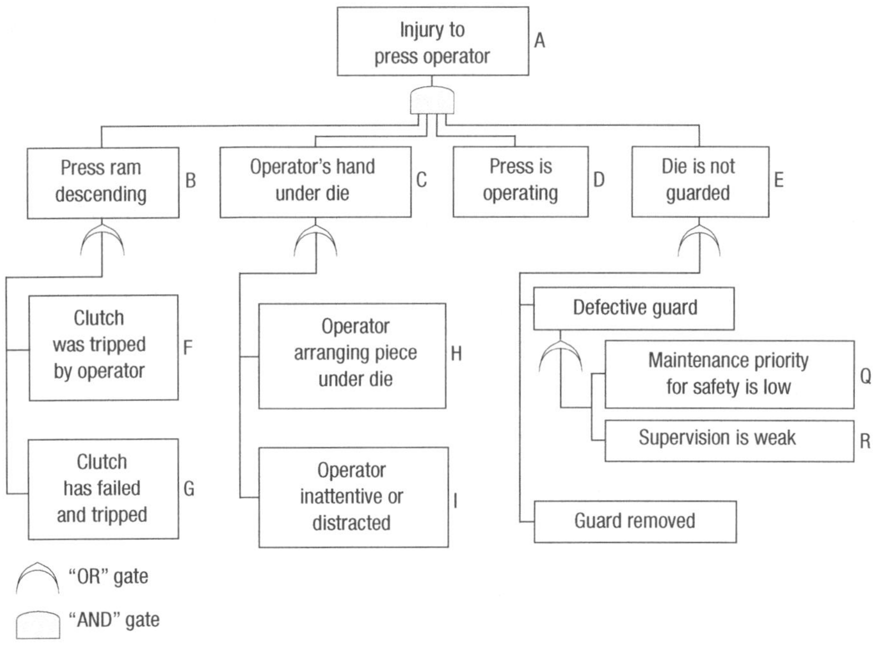

[DA12072]

Fault tree analysis, though, suffers from the same limitations as the traditional accident analysis techniques on which it is based. For example, if there is a high degree of uncertainty with underlying or base events, the probability of the accident may be difficult to ascertain. Additionally, important pathways to the accident might not be explored if some causal events are not included in the fault tree.

Traditional analysis also cannot easily account for human error (a significant contributor to construction accidents) and conditional failures (which cause one another in succession, culminating in an accident). As a result, and given the many combinations of hazards associated with construction sites, traditional analysis creates an incomplete, possibly inaccurate portrait of an accident's causation. Predictive models that incorporate on-site data gleaned from workers and their environment via sensors, however, promise to improve a risk manager's ability to incorporate such factors into the calculation of accident probability.

Sensor-Generated-Data Analysis Techniques

Wearables and other kinds of sensors are not new. From Holter monitors (wearable devices that use electrodes to record a patient's cardiac activity) to flight data recorders (which store an in-flight airplane's instrumentation measurements, electronic transmissions, and communications), information automatically captured at its source has always been essential to a precise retrospective rendering of an event. However, rapid advances in microprocessor capacity, battery miniaturization, and camera clarity have heralded a revolution in sensor and wearable technology, making products like these widely available:[2]

- Helmets that can identify toxic fumes or unsafe equipment
- Sensor-equipped shirts, wristbands, and skin patches that monitor a worker's stress level, respiration, heartbeat, energy output, body temperature, and hydration levels
- Assembly line sensors that adjust production speed based on worker attributes, fatigue levels, physical capabilities, and so on
- Footwear than can record a worker's footsteps, track his or her movements, and measure gait
- Head gear with embedded microchips that can detect brainwave activity that indicates a worker's fatigue level
- Vests that can detect unsafe worker body motion

Information harvested from workplace sensors and wearables is potentially useful in isolation—if, for example, an employee's wearable indicates an unsafe fatigue level or a machine sensor signals an impending malfunction. It is only fully useful, however, if relationships among accumulated data points illuminate the extent to which environmental conditions, worker attributes, and other relevant factors affect the probability of an accident occurring. This new information can be thought of as enhancing system safety analysis.

Consider a simple example of how, after sufficient data is collected from sensors, the construction contractor's risk manager can employ a classification tree model to determine the probability of a workplace accident. This technique is a form of supervised learning because it has a defined target variable of "Accident" or "Not accident."

First, data from each sensor is categorized and used to develop attributes that help predict workplace accidents. These attributes are combined with traditional workplace accident attributes, such as equipment failure or hours worked in a given shift. Each attribute is then analyzed independently for its information gain for predicting a workplace accident. See the exhibit "Sample of Worker and Environmental Attributes (Ranked by Information Gain)."

Sample of Worker and Environmental Attributes (Ranked by Information Gain)

Variable	Explanation
Hours worked shift	Number of hours worked on a given shift
Training gap	Number of days that have elapsed since worker's most recent training session
Equipment status	Numerical representation of equipment status, with 0 indicating an equipment failure and 1 indicating no equipment failure
Response time	Number of seconds it takes a worker to complete a given physical task
Body mass index	Worker's body mass index value
Consecutive days worked	Number of consecutive days a worker has recorded at least one hour of work time
Footsteps shift	Total number of footsteps a worker has taken during a given shift
Average resting pulse	Worker's average resting pulse rate during a given shift
Hydration level	Numerical representation of worker's hydration level on a scale of one to five, with five being best

[DA12073]

Then, a classification tree algorithm is applied to training data. Finally, hold-out data is used to test the model and determine its predictive power on data that was not used in model development.

The tree diagram's ovals represent the attributes under analysis, while the rectangles show the classification as "Accident" or "Not accident." Classification results from the combination of attributes connected to the rectangle through a sequence of arrows, each of which depicts the actual value of the attribute to which it is connected. Probabilities are added to each of the rectangles based on the percentage of times the model correctly predicts the specified class when applied to the training data. See the exhibit "Classification Tree Determined by Worker and Environmental Attribute Data."

The classification tree produced by the algorithm illustrates how various combinations of attributes can be used to predict the probability of an accident occurring. Understanding the manner in which various worker biological

Classification Tree Determined by Worker and Environmental Attribute Data

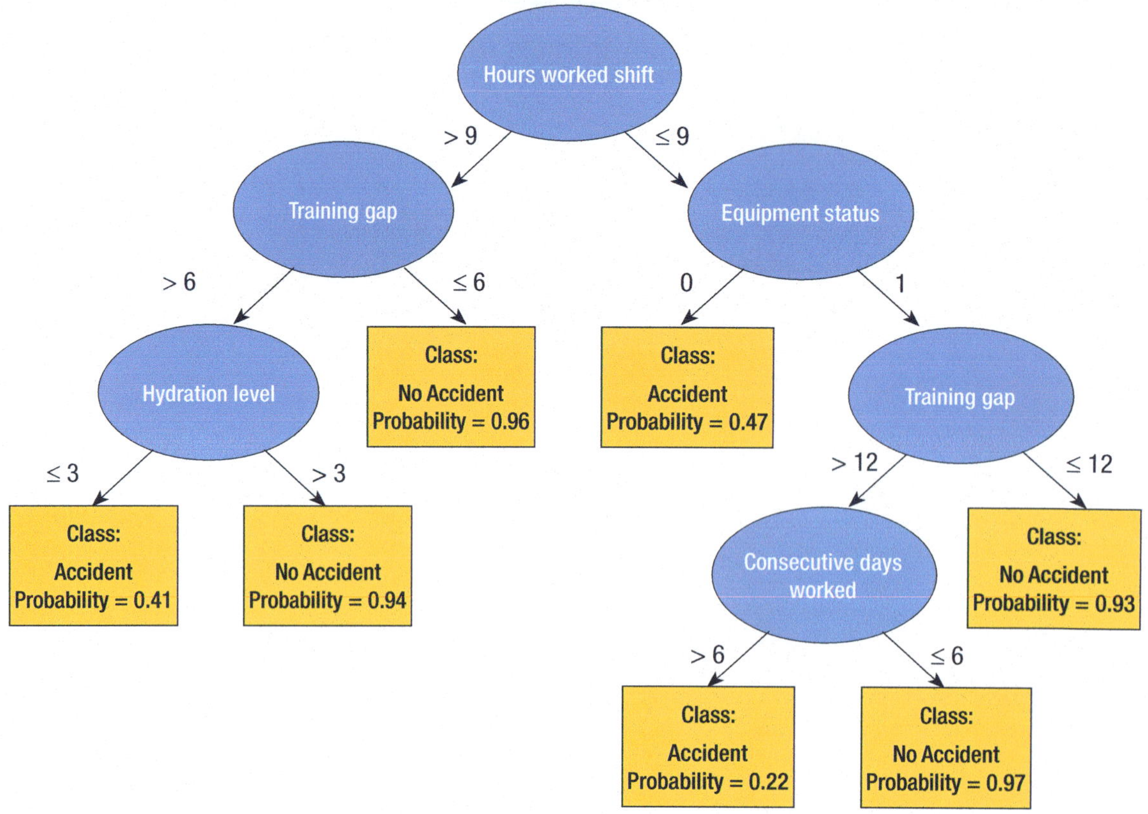

[DA12083]

traits, environmental factors, equipment failures, and other variables affect the probability of an accident occurring allows organizations to deploy risk management techniques, training regimens, labor divisions, and so forth to reduce associated accident probabilities.

Apply Your Knowledge

Which one of these statements best explains why classification tree analysis of accident probability is an example of a supervised learning technique?

a. The classification tree algorithm does not have a defined target variable.

b. The goal of the classification tree algorithm is to determine the probability of an accident occurring or not occurring.

c. The classification tree algorithm incorporates elements of traditional accident analysis techniques.

d. Probabilities of various combinations of factors combining to cause an accident are unknown.

Feedback: b. Classification tree analysis of accident probability is an example of a supervised learning technique because its goal is to determine the probability of an accident occurring or not occurring. Therefore, the classification tree algorithm's target variable is defined.

ASSESSING REPUTATION RISK THROUGH TEXT MINING AND SOCIAL NETWORK ANALYSIS

Reputation is an intangible asset that relates to an organization's goals and values, results from the behaviors and opinions of its stakeholders (stakeholder perception), and grows over time. It involves a comparison of stakeholders' experience and their expectations and is the pillar of the organization's legitimacy, or social license to operate.

For an organization to maintain a good reputation, it must earn and retain the trust and confidence of its key stakeholders. But how can an organization and its risk managers know when its stakeholders' trust and confidence are fading? Data analytics offers organizations a way to keep up to date on the shifting perceptions regarding their services and products.

Large clothing retailers typically receive their products from various manufacturers. While these manufacturers are external stakeholders of the retailers, they also represent a reputation risk. A retailer must consider not only its own actions but also how those of its manufacturers may affect the perceptions of the retailer's customers.

Suppose that Erin's Clothing, a large online retailer, has just learned that a news article is being published. The article reveals that Jones Incorporated, one of Erin's three primary clothing manufacturers, has been using underage laborers to produce its product. At the end of the article, a list of retailers that sell Jones's products appears, and Erin's is on the list. Erin's was not aware of the underage labor. Erin's is not the largest retailer named on the list, and Erin's senior management hopes that much of the press will be about the larger retailers. They ask Erin's risk manager to start assessing the situation.

The risk manager at Erin's knows that with today's instantaneous communication, a reputational crisis can compromise an organization in a matter of days or even hours. Immediately, the risk manager works with senior management to issue a statement emphasizing that Erin's will not tolerate underage labor from any of its manufacturers and announcing that it has terminated its relationship with Jones. However, the risk manager is still concerned about Jones's ability to affect Erin's reputation.

The risk manager would like to discover to what extent the news article is affecting stakeholders' opinions before taking more long-term reputation-related actions and/or releasing additional statements. Working with a team of data scientists, he will use text mining and social network analysis to come up with a plan of action.

Reputation Risk

Reputational risk
The risk that negative publicity, whether true or not, will damage a company's reputation and its ability to operate its business.

A systemic approach to **reputational risk** involves carefully managing the organization's interactions with the general public, its stakeholders, and its employees.

Social media provides a vehicle for any message to be instantaneously multiplied, expanded on, and communicated to millions of people. A single negative item of information—whether patently false, true, misinterpreted, or taken out of context—can reverse an organization's positive image and severely damage its reputation in a matter of hours, if not minutes.

Erin's risk manager is particularly concerned with how the underage labor story will affect Erin's reputation regarding its corporate social responsibility. These are the questions he wishes to address:

- Is the company viewed by its stakeholders as a good corporate citizen?
- Do the company's actions reflect its stakeholders' long-term interests?
- Does the company minimize the negative impact and maximize the positive impact of its business activities on the environment and society?

Text Mining

The first step the risk manager takes in the data mining process is to work with data scientists to mine news articles and social media posts for any mention in the past twenty-four hours (since the release of the initial news article) of "Erin's Clothing." The objective of this initial text mining project is to perform a sentiment analysis of those mentions.

To successfully analyze the text, it must first be cleaned up by eliminating spaces, punctuation, and words that provide little information, as well as by reducing words to their stems by removing prefixes and suffixes. The data scientists created two dictionaries: one with favorable words and another with unfavorable words related to the underage-labor situation.

Sometimes, the overall sentiment toward a statement can be difficult to determine. For example, someone might post, "The news about Jones Incorporated is awful. So sad. And Erin's is one of my favorite stores!" Is that a negative or positive mention of Erin's? It is both, and the computer could score the statement with a negative one for each negative sentiment and a positive one for each positive sentiment ($-1 + -1 + 1 = -1$). Sometimes statements result in a neutral score (typically zero), such as "Surprising news about Jones and Erin's."

The results of the sentiment analysis from news articles and social media posts indicate that the overall customer opinion of Erin's has indeed declined, with a much higher negative sentiment score than previously thought. However, the response appears to be mixed in terms of neutral or negative and in terms of what the negative sentiment is focused on, and the risk manager believes that it is worth investigating further to see how different demographic segments are reacting.

An analysis of the term frequency (TF) and inverse document frequency (IDF) of certain terms reveals additional insights. Most significantly, it shows that the sentiments expressed by younger consumers and youth-oriented press are more negative than those expressed by older consumers. Those younger consumers fall into two main categories: those posting about the tragedy of underage labor and those posting about their disgust with corporate greed. Stakeholders—customers and possibly employees—who live in the city where Erin's is headquartered seem to be especially upset by the news. The risk manager wants to know more about the sentiments of these hometown stakeholders.

The data scientists perform a TF analysis of a separate corpus consisting of recent opinion pieces and blog posts from Erin's home city that are geared toward younger consumers. The exhibit shows a simplified example with a limited number of documents. See the exhibit "Term Frequency Example: Erin's Clothing."

Term Frequency Example: Erin's Clothing

	Child(ren)	Immoral (synonyms included)	Underage	Greed (synonyms included)	Corporate
Document 1	4	2	3	0	1
Document 2	1	0	1	1	3
Document 3	2	3	4	1	0
Count	7	5	8	2	4

[DA12065]

Based on these results, the data scientists observe that the younger hometown population seems more concerned about the underage workers than about questioning the company's motives.

One term is used multiple times within only one of the blog posts. It has a high TF within that blog post and a high IDF, which is a measure of its rarity within the corpus of blogs. The combination of high TF within the blog post and high IDF indicates that the term is worthy of consideration. This term is "Springer," and Springer Attire is one of Erin's primary competitors. The author of the blog post is urging customers to shop there instead. It did not occur to the risk manager or the data scientists to search for the names of other online stores that do not sell Jones merchandise. The risk manager needs to consider how far and how quickly this article urging customers to shop elsewhere could spread.

Social Network Analysis

To fully understand the effect of the negative sentiment and how far-reaching the various posts and articles are, the risk manager and team of data scientists perform a social network analysis.

To analyze networks of this size and this amount of text, the risk manager uses a matrix. However, it is also useful to examine social network connections through a sociogram to understand how far a negative sentiment that originates with one person or a few people can spread. The "Negative Sentiment in a Network" exhibit shows the walks of the negative sentiment as it passes from node to node (person to person). The influence of the negative sentiment significantly depends on its posters' **degree**, **closeness**, and **betweenness**. See the exhibit "Negative Sentiment in a Network."

Degree

The measure of the number of connections each node has.

Closeness

The measure of the average distance, or path length, between a particular node and the other nodes in a network.

Betweenness

The measure of how many times a particular node is part of the shortest path between two other nodes in a network.

Negative Sentiment in a Network

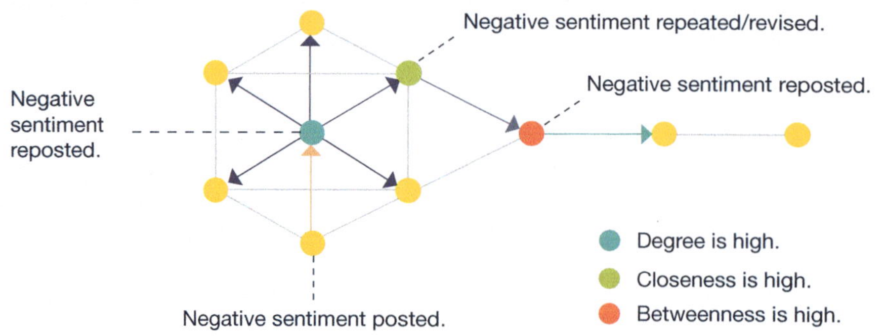

[DA12066]

The centrality measures of degree, closeness, and betweenness matter not only in the context of one network, but also in the context of how one person or a few people can connect multiple social media networks. As shown in the "Connections Among Social Networks" exhibit, by targeting stakeholders in Social Network C, Erin's message will most likely flow to the other social networks. The risk manager can also see that certain individuals from Social Network B have high betweenness. While it would be ethically questionable and not particularly worthwhile to target individuals, Erin's should target messaging to Social Network B in addition to Social Network C. See the exhibit "Connections Among Social Networks."

Connections Among Social Networks

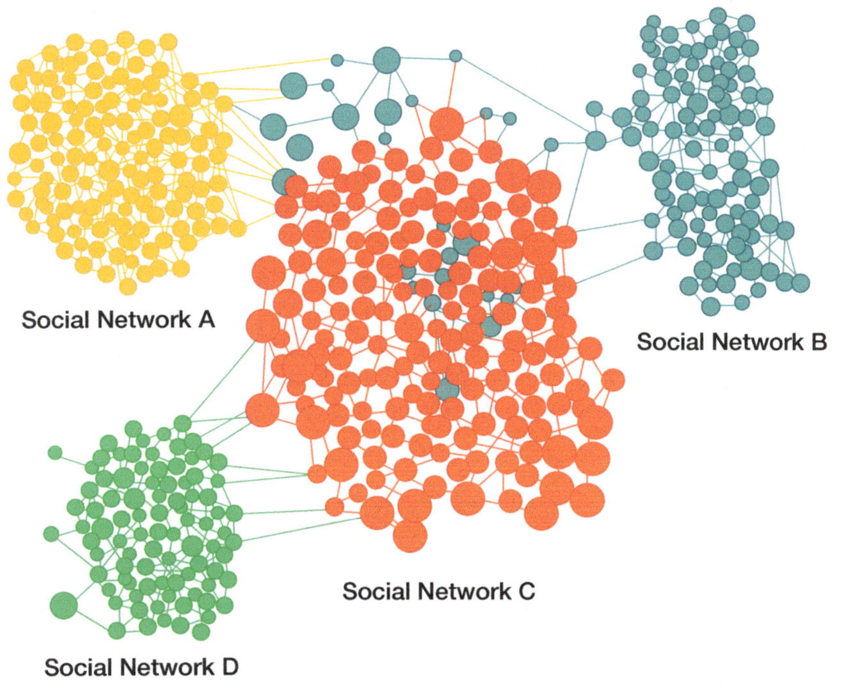

[DA12067]

By considering the combination of the local variables of age and location and the network variables of degree, closeness, and betweenness, as well as the intensity of the social network interactions, the data scientists and the risk manager can better target their responses to the crisis. Erin's risk manager realizes that the negative sentiment has spread far in a short period of time and that he must implement an immediate and sufficient risk response.

Erin's takes the initiative to post educational articles and videos regarding underage labor and to provide a list of resources for those who would like to know more or contribute to the cause of ending it. Because Erin's has performed a text mining and social network analysis, it knows the most influential places to post this material and focuses primarily on younger consumers and on stakeholders living near Erin's headquarters. A follow-up sentiment analysis reveals that Erin's reputation has begun to improve. Going forward, Erin's risk manager will carefully monitor the organization's reputation so that he can quickly respond to any growing negative sentiment expressed in print or online. See the exhibit "Privacy Concerns Regarding Network Analysis."

Privacy Concerns Regarding Network Analysis

When performing a social network analysis, businesses must be aware of and sensitive to their stakeholders' privacy concerns. They also need to carefully investigate any privacy regulations that apply in the countries and states in which they are doing business.

Ideally, organizations should be interested in the flow of data and should take precautions not to specifically identify individual customers. Most customers/stakeholders would not take kindly to having information about them pieced together from various sources and made available to commercial organizations. This, in itself, is a reputation risk.

The process of obscuring individual information is not as simple as it may seem. Even if an organization removes personal identifiers from its data, those seeking the information can piece someone's identity together from various databases. Data scientists continue to work on developing new ways to ensure individuals' privacy while still allowing organizations to reap the benefits of network analysis.

[DA12068]

Apply Your Knowledge

What are the benefits of performing a social network analysis in combination with or directly after performing text mining of social media?

Feedback: Performing a network analysis can provide information about how far and how quickly a sentiment has and could spread.

USING CLUSTERING AND LINEAR MODELING FOR LOSS DEVELOPMENT

Long-tail claim

A claim in which there is a duration of more than one year from the date of loss to closure.

Ultimate loss

The final paid amount for all losses in an accident year.

Estimating losses accurately is fundamental to assessing the financial status of an organization. **Long-tail claims** can be difficult to predict, as they are complex claims that involve multiple factors. Big data analysis techniques can improve the accuracy of predictions of the **ultimate losses** for such claims.

It is important for risk management professionals to understand how data analysis techniques can improve the accuracy of loss development predictions, which have a significant financial effect on an organization. For example, self-insured organizations must show loss estimates as liabilities on their balance sheets. An organization's reserves to pay future losses affect the amount of capital that the organization can deploy for projects such as business expansion. Applying data analysis techniques to losses, especially to long-tail claims, can improve the accuracy of loss development estimates and thereby help risk management professionals make better business decisions.

Diane, the risk manager at a large, self-insured organization, is working on a project to identify factors involved in the development of general liability losses. The organization self-insures the first $100,000 of each loss occurrence and purchases **excess liability insurance** above that amount. **Adverse development** of the self-insured losses has been an ongoing concern for the chief financial officer. Diane has identified slips and falls as the category of general liability claims that is responsible for most of the adverse development, and she has worked with the safety team on preventive techniques. However, although slip-and-fall accidents are occurring less frequently, the severity of these claims has increased.

Excess liability insurance

Insurance coverage for losses that exceed the limits of underlying insurance coverage or a retention amount.

Adverse development

Increasing claims costs for which the reserves are inadequate.

Overview of the Procedure

Estimating hazard losses (dollar amounts) entails calculating an estimate of ultimate losses for specific accident years. These predictions are based on total **incurred losses** at various intervals after the beginning of the accident year in which the losses occurred, such as eighteen, thirty, forty-two, and fifty-four months. General liability losses are typically assumed to reach their ultimate value within sixty-six months. Loss development factors, usually based on previous accident years' loss development data, are multiplied by the total incurred losses for each accident year to reach an estimate of the ultimate loss for that year. For example, if the total incurred loss at eighteen months was $500,000 and a loss development factor of 2 was used, the prediction of the ultimate loss would be $1 million.

Incurred losses

The sum of paid losses, paid loss adjustment expenses, loss reserves, and loss adjustment expense reserves.

Diane plans to identify the reasons why the previous loss predictions were underestimated. To accomplish this, she will follow these steps:

- Collect and organize past data
- Apply data analysis techniques
- Develop a more accurate method to predict severity of losses

Collect and Organize Past Data

Diane develops a database of five years of closed slip-and-fall claims. By definition, a closed claim is assumed to have reached its ultimate value. She also compares the previous estimates valued at eighteen months after the beginning of each accident year with the actual ultimate results. See the exhibit "Comparison of General Liability Loss Estimates to Actual Ultimate Losses."

Apply Data Analysis Techniques

Diane works with the organization's data scientist, Jill, to develop an approach to analyzing the slip-and-fall claims. Because they do not understand the factors that have caused the adverse development, Jill recommends applying k-means cluster analysis, an unsupervised learning technique. As a result of the analysis, they discover an outlier cluster of claims based on claims size and

Comparison of General Liability Loss Estimates to Actual Ultimate Losses

Accident Year	Estimate of Ultimate Losses (,000)*	Actual Ultimate Losses (,000)
20X1	$3,061	$15,050
20X2	$4,232	$17,304
20X3	$3,114	$18,876
20X4	$2,356	$19,114
20X5	$2,209	$22,407

*Valued at 18 months after the beginning of the accident year.

[DA12071]

the ratio of ultimate incurred loss to incurred loss at the eighteen-month evaluation point. See the exhibit "Cluster Analysis of General Liability Claims."

Cluster Analysis of General Liability Claims

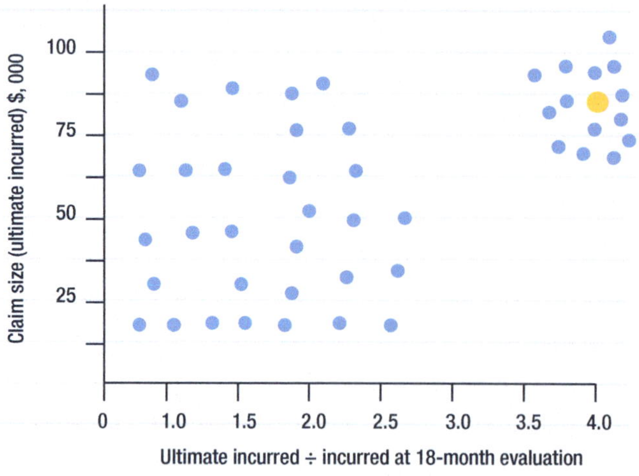

[DA12076]

The outlier cluster is characterized by high severity (limited by the $100,000 self-insurance amount) and a high ratio (≥3.5) of the ultimate incurred value to the incurred value at eighteen months. The claims in this cluster were underreserved to a much greater degree at eighteen months than were the other claims that were analyzed.

Diane and Jill examine the claims in the outlier cluster and discover that aside from having attributes in common with other high-severity claims, the outliers share these additional attributes:

- Reported more than one week after the date of the accident
- Liability denied by the claims representative
- Claimant represented by an attorney

Working with an outside actuary, Jill then used a generalized linear model(GLM) to project the average ultimate severity as the target variable for these types of claims based on their attributes. This is a supervised learning technique. The average ultimate severity was then used to set the incurred claims amounts at the eighteen-month evaluation point.

Develop a More Accurate Method to Predict Losses

Diane believes that the claims in which liability was denied were likely under-reserved because the claims representatives' outlook that the denials would be upheld was too optimistic. In fact, these claims were often of the highest severity because of large jury awards. Additionally, significant litigation expenses were involved.

Diane discusses her findings with the team manager at the third-party administrator that handles her organization's claims. She recommends a more thorough investigation into potential liability before a claim is denied. She also requests that the claim reserves be based on the results of the GLM.

Diane meets with the organization's safety director to discuss the importance of prompt reporting of all accidents with a focus on slips and falls. She recommends a policy of reporting all incidents, no matter how minor they might seem at the time, that have the potential to develop into a claim. She also recommends that the safety department continue to work on ways to prevent slips and falls.

In the future, after the preceding changes have taken effect, the analysis will need to be repeated to determine whether outlier claims are still disproportionately contributing to adverse development. If not, the accuracy of estimated ultimate losses at the eighteen-month evaluation point should improve considerably.

SUMMARY

Workplace accidents and their causes are ideal subjects for the application of data analytics techniques because traditional methods of workplace accident analysis rely on human interpretation of limited amounts of information and cannot always account for how contributing factors combine to cause an accident. Data collected from wearables can help create predictive models that use relationships among myriad variables to improve the accuracy of predictions about accidents and identify the best ways to stop them.

An organization can help manage its reputation risk by using data mining techniques to discover the sentiment behind social media posts and by analyzing how that sentiment spreads in a social network. With this knowledge, risk managers can more effectively respond to reputation risks.

It is important for risk management professionals to determine the ultimate value of losses as accurately as possible. Data analysis techniques can be applied to loss data to understand factors that contribute to underreserving and better predict ultimate losses. Additionally, data analysis can help identify the factors involved in high-severity claims in order to support development of better safety solutions and claims handling procedures.

ASSIGNMENT NOTES

1. United States Department of Labor, "Worker Safety Series: Construction," OSHA 3252-05N 2005, https://www.osha.gov/Publications/OSHA3252/3252.html (accessed June 29, 2016).
2. Michelle Kerr, "Putting Wearables to Work," Risk & Insurance, June 1, 2015, www.riskandinsurance.com/putting-wearables-to-work/ (accessed June 27, 2016).

Direct Your Learning

9

Implementing a Data Analytics Strategy

Educational Objectives

After learning the content of this assignment, you should be able to:

- Explain how an organization can apply SWOT analysis to develop a data analytics strategy.
- Explain how an organization can apply the enterprise risk management process to a data analytics project.
- Explain how an organization can apply the change management process when implementing a data analytics strategy.

Outline

Implementing a Data Analytics Strategy

9

DATA ANALYTICS STRATEGY

It's no surprise that the property-casualty insurance industry, rooted in risk aversion and predicated on long-term stability, has traditionally been slow to embrace change. An insurer that anticipates a fundamental shift in how business is conducted—such as that wrought by the emergence of data analytics—can therefore potentially gain a marketplace edge by adopting new practices more quickly or efficiently than its competitors.

An organization's integration of data analytics begins with its acceptance of the fundamental concept that more decision-making information, used intelligently, is always better. Then it's a matter of determining which aspects of the operation would most benefit from the insights that using data analytics may provide. One way an insurer can determine this is to perform a **SWOT analysis** (or situational analysis).

SWOT analysis

A method of evaluating the internal and external environments by assessing an organization's internal strengths and weaknesses and its external opportunities and threats.

A SWOT (strengths, weaknesses, opportunities, and threats) analysis allows an organization to consider both the general environment and its immediate environment. The method was devised by Albert S. Humphrey, a business scholar and management consultant who specialized in business planning and change. The approach used by organizations varies based on each company's needs. A company should not only identify strengths, weaknesses, opportunities, and threats, but also thoroughly analyze how they affect its strategic plan. See the exhibit "SWOT Analysis Table."

SWOT Analysis Table

	Strengths	Weaknesses
Internal	List assets, competencies, or attributes that enhance competitiveness Prioritize based on the quality of the strength and the relative importance of the strength	List lacking assets, competencies, or attributes that diminish competitiveness Prioritize based on the seriousness of the weakness and the relative importance of the weakness
	Opportunities	**Threats**
External	List conditions that could be exploited to create a competitive advantage Prioritize based on the potential of exploiting the opportunities	List conditions that diminish competitive advantage Prioritize based on the seriousness and probability of occurrence
	Note strengths that can be paired with opportunities as areas of competitive advantage	Note weaknesses that can be paired with threats as risks to be avoided

[DA03626]

Because an organization's strategies can be extensive, it is helpful to narrow the focus of a SWOT analysis by understanding the business issue that has prompted the evaluation. The strategies relevant to the issue can then be targeted for evaluation. In this case, a SWOT analysis focused specifically on the potential use of data analytics enables management to develop two general perspectives:

- Internal (organizational) strengths and weaknesses that could potentially be affected by a data analytics initiative—Identifying internal strengths and weaknesses involves consideration of financial, physical, human, and organizational assets.[1] Managers use SWOT analysis to determine the current state of their organizations based on factors like managerial expertise, available product lines, staff competencies, current strategies, customer loyalty, growth levels, organizational structure, and distribution channels.
- External factors that present opportunities for growth or threats to the organization's survival—One way to achieve this perspective is through trend analysis, which identifies patterns related to specific factors in the past and then projects those patterns into the future to determine potential threats or opportunities. Opportunities might be presented by new markets, possible acquisition targets, or a reduction in competition, while threats might include new competitors, an increase in competition levels, economic downturns, or changes in customer preferences.

Let's examine how a hypothetical property-casualty insurer, Millstone Insurance, might use a SWOT analysis as the genesis of its data analytics strategy. Millstone spent decades building a brand that consumers associated with reasonable costs and personalized service. Recently, though, Millstone's once-dominant market share has crumbled beneath the weight of its competitors' superior pricing and its own deteriorating loss experience. Management is concerned about not only the durability of Millstone's cost leadership strategy, but also its ability to continue offering the superior service its customers expect in an increasingly competitive environment. It realizes that the insurer's survival may hinge on its ability to develop new competitive edges. Is a data analytics initiative the solution? See the exhibit "SWOT Analysis Process."

SWOT Analysis Process

One method of conducting a SWOT analysis is through a group activity that involves an organization's managers and is organized by a facilitator.

Brainstorming

- If the group is large, the facilitator may divide the managers into smaller groups to encourage participation.
- Through brainstorming, factors are listed under each of the SWOT headings.
- This activity will produce many factors randomly organized under each SWOT heading.

Refining

- To make the list easier to examine, similar items are clustered together.
- Items of high importance are noted under each of the SWOT headings.

Prioritizing

- Strengths are ordered by quality and relative importance.
- Weaknesses are ordered by the degree to which they affect performance and by their relative importance.
- Opportunities are ordered by degree and probability of success.
- Threats are ordered by degree and probability of occurrence.
- Strengths that require little or no operational changes and can be paired with opportunities are designated for potential action to maximize competitive advantages that entail low risk.
- Weaknesses that can be paired with threats are designated in the prioritized list for potential action to minimize consequences that entail high risk.

[DA03650]

Millstone's approach to its data-oriented SWOT analysis creates the foundation on which it can build its new initiative—targeting data analytics techniques toward three related ends:

- Reinforcing the strengths inherent in its business strategy (cost leadership)
- Mitigating threats and weaknesses
- Exploiting opportunities

Reinforcing Strengths

Determining how the use of data analytics could reinforce the strengths inherent in Millstone's business strategy means first understanding the key components of that strategy.

At Millstone's inception, its research suggested that a significant segment of its potential customers would switch insurers if they thought doing so would save them money, even if they believed they were risking poorer service. So, Millstone's founders gambled that guaranteeing lower premiums than its main competitors—a cost leadership strategy—would help the insurer quickly distinguish itself in a crowded market.

Millstone concluded that it could sustain its signature low rates in two significant ways:

- Reducing the costs of the product—Like all insurers, Millstone has operating expenses that include underwriting costs, claims expenses, taxes, and other fees. Some of these costs are difficult or impossible to control, but insurers can take steps to reduce many of them through claims management and operating expense management.
- Increasing profitable business—Through effective product management, Millstone has segmented its business to maximize underwriting results. It also identifies its most profitable risks and focuses its marketing efforts on those targets.

Millstone's cost leadership strategy led to its cultivation of a customer base that has remained loyal for many years. Here's some evidence that Millstone's strategy resonates in this market niche:

- Recent market research indicates that most consumers associate Millstone with inexpensive coverage and excellent customer service, despite Millstone's relatively small investment in advertising.
- Millstone's vast network of agencies is coordinated to provide personalized service to insureds and is especially adept at expediting claims resolution.
- Millstone's emphasis on quick, fair claims resolution has become the industry benchmark for responsiveness.

The investment required to launch a data analytics initiative could undermine Millstone's cost reduction strategy. For instance, the costs required to implement machine learning techniques could dwarf Millstone's current data-related expenditures. And personnel capable of executing data analytics strategies cost money to recruit, train, and retain.

Reinforcing its strengths, then, requires Millstone to maximize its data analytics investment by increasing its profitable business, although some opportunities may lie in reducing costs as well. The specific ways in which it might do so are revealed in Millstone's analysis of the connection among the other three SWOT elements: weaknesses, opportunities, and threats.

Mitigating Weaknesses and Threats

Pervasive brand recognition and enviable customer retention levels are not enough to eclipse Millstone's two most significant problems: its competitors' targeting its most profitable segments by offering lower premiums and its steadily deteriorating loss experience. Here are some of the internal weaknesses that management thinks may have contributed to this disastrous combination:

- Failure to quickly identify increasingly frequent and costly fraudulent claims whose cumulative effect on Millstone's loss ratio has become too significant to ignore
- Inability to discern which characteristics or combination of characteristics present in Millstone's book of business; its underwriting guidelines; and, by extension, its loss ratio could be contributing to its diminishing profitability
- Existence of an environment that discourages unconventional, analytical solutions to problems

How could a data analytics initiative help Millstone mitigate its internal weaknesses and external threats? See the exhibit "Using Data Analytics to Mitigate Weaknesses."

Exploiting Opportunities

Increased competition is not Millstone's only external worry. These are some of the technological, sociological, and industry trends that could fundamentally change the way Millstone does business:

- Recruitment and retention challenges posed by the scarcity of new workers entering the industry.
- Customers' increased access to information about competitors' prices ultimately could force Millstone to lower prices even more to remain viable in its market niche.
- Increasingly cynical public attitudes about insurers, fueled by online communication, create a more permissive environment for claims fraud.

Using Data Analytics to Mitigate Weaknesses

Weakness/Threat	Data Analytics Solution
Inability to identify fraudulent claims	Millstone could more intelligently deploy its special investigation unit (SIU) by using predictive modeling to prioritize a claim for investigation based on the probability that it is fraudulent. In this case, predictive models would rely on data mining techniques such as text mining, social network analysis, and cluster analysis to refine Millstone's insights about characteristics of potentially fraudulent claims and/or suspicious claimants.
Diminishing effectiveness of existing policy segmentation methods	Machine learning, from which patterns are recognized in Millstone's book of business, underwriting guidelines, and loss ratio, could allow for more finely honed policy segmentation and underwriting guidelines that lead to optimized pricing, better coverage decisions, and an improved marketing focus. A fully trained segmentation model can find meaningful patterns in data and automatically segment policies. This capability allows underwriters to analyze the segmentation and make more-informed rate changes, which improves loss ratios and customer retention.
Pervasive conventional thinking	Merely beginning to use data analytics techniques is not enough to overcome the influence of stagnant ideas. Millstone's data analytics initiative can succeed only if the entire organization understands the value of intelligently deployed information and everyone begins to consider how they can apply data-driven decision making.

[DA12043]

How could a data analytics initiative help Millstone exploit opportunities presented by the external environment? See the exhibit "Using Data Analytics to Exploit Opportunities."

Using Data Analytics to Exploit Opportunities

Opportunity	Data Analytics Solution
Scarcity of new workers willing to enter the insurance industry	A philosophical shift in Millstone's decision-making processes could, if extended even to its human resources department, allow it to develop novel approaches to attracting and retaining new employees. For example, Millstone could focus recruitment efforts on students majoring in mathematics, computer science, and data analytics by representing itself as a chance for them to use their skills in a cutting-edge organization at the forefront of a socially conscious industry. Additionally, Millstone could use predictive modeling techniques to develop the ability to analyze employee turnover and hiring patterns to determine recruits most likely to stay with the company, how to incentivize employees to remain engaged, and so forth.
Customers' increased access to information about competitors' prices	In addition to using data analytics methods to more precisely segment its policies, Millstone could use social network analysis, text mining, and other techniques to accumulate as much publicly available intelligence about its competitors as possible.
Cynical public attitudes about insurers	Millstone could use sentiment analysis algorithms, social network analysis, and other means of measuring the extent to which public attitudes about its coverage and about insurance in general could contribute to an insured's propensity to file a fraudulent claim.

[DA12044]

DATA ANALYTICS RISK MANAGEMENT

Data analytics alone does not sharpen an organization's competitive advantage or improve its ability to manage risks. In fact, the volume, velocity, and variety of readily available data mean that a poorly managed data analytics initiative can turn a stream of potentially useful information into a tsunami of data stripped of useful context. Therefore, the process an organization uses to implement a data analytics project and manage its inherent risks is just as important as the initiative itself.

Ideally, an organization should manage the risks associated with a data analytics project with the same discipline it applies to managing its other risks. One way to do this is through project risk management. Project risk management aims to optimize risk levels to achieve the project goal. Its underlying structured process allows risk managers to identify and assess a project's risks and to respond appropriately.

The enterprise risk management (ERM) process model illustrates the interconnected flow of a project's risk management activities in five steps. By applying the ERM process to a project, an organization synchronizes its overall risk management with the strategic goals and operational objectives of that specific project. See the exhibit "Enterprise Risk Management Process Model."

Enterprise Risk Management Process Model

[DA08717_2]

Consider an organization that wants to use data analytics to more effectively manage its supply chain. Think of a supply chain as branches of a tree connected to one another through a common trunk. Supply chain management entails assessing and mitigating all the threats that might interrupt the normal flow of goods and services from and to an organization's stakeholders. When applied to the production of goods, supply chain risk management encompasses managing the volatility related to producing, transporting, and storing goods, as well as managing the distribution channels from the initial raw materials to the final consumer product. Disruptions in an organization's production affect its immediate financial condition and may irreparably damage its brand reputation.

The organization wants to use sensors and social networking data to maximize its supply chain's efficiency and mitigate associated risks. It envisions developing a system in which such data provides real-time assessments of inventory levels, logistical issues connected to the movement of goods from one point on the chain to the next, fluctuations in pricing, shifts in customer sentiments, and other crucial information. The organization begins to realize the magnitude of this ambition and asks its risk manager to determine the potential pitfalls that could undermine the project's implementation by applying each step of the ERM process model:

- Scan environment
- Identify risks
- Analyze risks
- Treat risks
- Monitor and assure

Scan Environment

The risk manager first needs to develop a sense of how the organization's data analytics initiative will merge with its existing infrastructure and how the project could affect the organization's stakeholders. This can be accomplished with an analysis of the organization's internal and external environments.

Internal Environment

The risk manager's consideration of the internal environment begins with clarifying the objective of the data analytics project. While the overarching goal of using sensor and social networking data to improve supply chain efficiencies is a feasible starting point for the project, the more specific an initiative's objective, the easier it is for the risk manager to anticipate risks, analyze hypothetical scenarios, measure success, and so forth.

To hone the project's goal, the risk manager could interview various internal stakeholders and develop a series of quantifiable objectives that, together, constitute the project's overall goal. These could include, for example, (1) using sensor data and vehicle telematics from supply truck drivers to determine the most efficient way to divide shift work based on driver fatigue, (2) using continuous updates about inventory levels to best calibrate supply shipments, and (3) mining social networking data to discern economic and political trends that could affect a foreign supply point's viability. The risk manager also has to consider internal factors such as the amount and types of risk involved, key strategies, and available resources.

One potential problem on which the risk manager focuses in this instance is the necessity to extensively train employees, hire data scientists and people capable of analyzing large amounts of data, and acquire new technology, including sensors at all points on the supply chain and information technology upgrades. Reviewing the available resources could determine whether contingency funds are available or whether additional costs could undermine the project's profitability.

External Environment

The organization's external environment includes technological, economic, legal and regulatory, political, natural, and competitive factors that could affect the project. Here are examples of how some of these factors could undermine the data analytics project under consideration:

- Technological—Reliance on sensors, many of which need to be installed in remote locations along the organization's supply chain, requires the organization to ensure that the sensors are properly maintained and consistently dependable. Ineffective or improperly located sensors may supply compromised or even misleading data that could jeopardize the initiative.
- Legal and regulatory—The risk manager may have to consider legal and regulatory issues associated with the use of employees' and contractors' personal data and the mining of social networking websites. For example, if one of the organization's primary distribution centers is located in a country with relatively restrictive regulations regarding Internet use, investing in social network data mining may not be worthwhile.
- Political—Just as the risk manager must be attuned to the legal and regulatory concerns associated with each point on the supply chain, he or she must also consider political risks, which vary by location. For example, labor unions in a particular region might encourage their members to resist wearing sensors that track their whereabouts, footsteps, and vital signs.

Identify Risks

While it is not feasible or practical for the risk manager to identify all of the risks associated with the data analytics project, it is important to identify key and emerging risks. The primary concern is determining which potential risks will require treatment. For example, mining social networking data might have initially been viewed as potentially useful at supply chain points with hospitable regulatory and political climates, but it can also be seen as a risk to the company's reputation if media reports depict the organization as invading personal privacy for profit.

Analyze Risks

Risk analysis attempts to determine the source, cause, likelihood, and potential consequences of each identified risk. One method of assessing risks in the data analytics project is to identify component activities of the project and then examine the risks associated with each activity's tasks. In doing this, the parameters for each activity—such as time estimates, costs, quality measurements, staff requirements, and predecessor activities—are reviewed to determine what variances are acceptable while still achieving the project goals.

Examples of the component activities associated with the data analytics initiative include these:

- Alignment of the data analytics project's goals with upper management's long-term organizational objectives
- Recruitment of data scientists and support personnel
- Determination of the specific categories of data the project intends to analyze
- Identification of the means of acquiring the necessary data
- Installation of sensors and other means of data acquisition at crucial points in the supply chain
- Development of a strategy to inform affected employees about the initiative and encourage their participation

During this assessment, the time estimates for crucial activities should be scrutinized, because any risk can potentially extend the project's final completion date. Acceptable variances for each activity become the basis for analyzing foreseeable risks that can cause results to fall outside the acceptable parameters. For each activity and associated task, the risk manager judges the likelihood and severity of the impact on the project. The project team can then prioritize risks according to the risks' potential to negatively affect project results. Any risk to activities deemed likely to extend the project beyond its completion date receives a higher priority for treatment.

Treat Risks

Once risks to the data analytics project are prioritized, the risk manager considers risk management techniques for addressing them and implements the best technique or combination of techniques for each. The most effective technique or techniques for managing a risk are determined by considering how the risk might affect the project's successful completion. The techniques selected should create a risk outcome that is within acceptable variances.

Some of the major options for treating risk are avoidance, modification, transfer, retention, or exploitation. However, opportunities that accompany risk should not be overlooked. In this case, including a new technique for mining social media data that, despite being costly, will ultimately continue to save the company money in both implementation time and energy costs may provide a great opportunity that more than offsets the risk.

In addition to using risk management techniques, project teams address risks through contingency planning, which involves establishing alternative procedures for possible events. The alternative procedures are established in advance and should be within the variance requirement of each activity. Contingency planning facilitates keeping the entire project on track within the project constraints.

Monitor and Assure

As the data analytics initiative progresses, the project manager compares the quality, time, budget, and other constraints established in the project's scope statement with the project status. The variances established for each activity are useful in determining whether individual activities are progressing within acceptable parameters.

The project manager must also monitor progression of the entire project to determine whether the project goal will be achieved. For example, each activity might be at maximum variance with its budget allocation. Any significant additional expense could push the entire project outside its budget constraints. If a project is reasonably within budget, the project manager might reallocate resources from less-critical activities to activities with greater resource requirements.

DATA ANALYTICS CHANGE MANAGEMENT

Nearly all insurers have incorporated at least some elements of data analytics into their decision making. But as the internet continues to fundamentally alter consumer expectations and the volume and variety of available data keep exponentially increasing, insurers that don't have a comprehensive data analytics strategy are destined to realize its importance too late. So how can an insurer, typically dependent on legacy systems and risk-averse business philosophies, survive the change necessary to become a data-driven organization?

An insurer's evolution from adhering to its traditional roots to using data analytics as the foundation of its decision making is a complex undertaking best implemented through the change management process. See the exhibit "The Change Management Process."

The Change Management Process

1. Articulate the need for change
2. Appoint a leadership team
3. Develop a written statement of the vision and strategies
4. Communicate the vision and strategies
5. Eliminate barriers to change
6. Recognize incremental successes
7. Entrench the change

[DA12057]

The steps in the change management process might appear to be simple, but each one takes significant effort to accomplish without undermining or derailing the process. This is especially relevant for insurers when the change entails a fundamental shift in philosophy, such as the one from reliance on traditional organizational infrastructures to data-driven analysis.

Articulate the Need for Change

When an organization recognizes that it needs to change, it first has to articulate why. That's because the manner in which the need for change is expressed throughout the organization affects how a proposed change is received. It's not enough for upper management to simply mandate the shift to data-driven processes. Instead, it must first inspire organization-wide engagement by demonstrating that introducing more decision-making information to as many processes as possible is not just better but is essential to the insurer's ability to maintain its market share as competitors use data analytics techniques to improve their underwriting, pricing, fraud detection, and marketing.

Framing this shift as being crucial to the insurer's ability to acquire and retain business is the most effective way to impart a sense of urgency to the change. A sense of urgency helps persuade key individuals to invest in the change and creates the momentum required to spur the organization to action. Reasons for urgency must be supportable; if people perceive the urgency as false or exaggerated, they may withhold support for change.

Appoint a Leadership Team

Major transformations are usually associated with one highly visible change agent and a collaborative team of sponsors of the change, referred to as the leadership team. The leadership team is made up of carefully selected individuals who recognize the need for the change and provide solid, broad-based support for accomplishing it. The change agent and leadership team should have the credibility and authority to take action, obtain resources, and direct others' actions.

One way an insurer may execute this step is to designate a leadership team known as a center of excellence (COE), which addresses the need for a combination of strong business leadership and data analytics leadership.[2] A COE consists of personnel dedicated solely to developing data analytics strategies, formulating department-specific data analytics goals, implementing plans to encourage organization-wide collaboration on data analytics initiatives, and overseeing the evolution of a data analytics model from concept to adoption.

Essentially, members of the insurer's COE are responsible for creating the vision of the change and selling it to others. Therefore, members of the COE should have the power to eliminate any obstacles to progress, expertise relevant to the change, the credibility to convince others that the need for change should be taken seriously, and leadership to catalyze the change process.

Develop a Written Statement of the Vision and Strategies

An insurer's data analytics initiative should be guided by a vision statement that is realistic, desirable, feasible, motivational, and focused enough to guide decision making. This statement also needs to be communicated readily; without a clearly articulated vision, the transformation to a data-driven organization can dissolve into a tangle of confusing, incompatible, time-consuming, and counterproductive projects.

A common error is to mistake plans and programs for an appropriate vision. For example, some organizations assume that actions focused on training, team creation, and other activities that should produce positive results constitute a vision. However, a vision should succinctly align, direct, and inspire collective action toward a common end point that improves the organization's measurable results. See the exhibit "Sample Data Analytics Vision Statement."

Sample Data Analytics Vision Statement

We will incorporate data analytics into all of our major decision-making processes within five years. Achieving this goal will require that data-driven philosophies permeate all facets of the organization, from senior management discussions to interactions with individual customers. We will improve our ratemaking through telematics, refine our underwriting through data mining, and use business process analytics to improve our claims processes.

[DA12058]

Here are some of the qualities of an effective vision statement for a data analytics initiative:

- It provides a general direction for improving the organization's products, services, cost control, and/or relationships with customers and stakeholders.
- It can be clearly described in five minutes or less.
- It considers trends in technology and the market.
- It is stated in positive terms.

Communicate the Vision and Strategies

The COE, with the support of the insurer's decision makers, then communicates the overarching vision and the main supporting strategies to all employees using multiple forums to ensure that everyone sees and hears the message repeatedly and consistently.

If a vision is not communicated sufficiently, employees may prefer the status quo, particularly with an endeavor such as a data analytics initiative, which directly confronts traditional, deeply ingrained organizational practices and ideas. Communicating the vision with an appropriate level of urgency may require removing sources of complacency or reducing their impact. Those tasks can be as simple as effectively countering expected arguments or as complicated as eliminating signals that are contrary to the message.

Eliminate Barriers to Change

Becoming a data-driven insurer involves many people from all levels of the organization. Therefore, everyone must be empowered to become a part of the process and to understand the relevance of the change. However, employees cannot effect change if barriers prohibit action. They may embrace the vision but feel disempowered by real or perceived obstacles.

To eliminate barriers to change, upper management and the COE should use the momentum of the change process to alter the systems, structures, and policies that are inconsistent with the vision and strategies. Such barriers can appear in forms including these:[3]

- Technological entanglements that limit change, such as legacy computer, data collection, and communication systems that discourage interaction among departments
- Absence among existing personnel of skills necessary to understand, apply, and interpret results derived from data analytics techniques
- An organizational culture that doesn't value data analytics capabilities or methods
- Inappropriately ambitious timelines for implementing data analytics techniques that, if unmet, could lead to skepticism about the overall endeavor

Recognize Incremental Successes

The leadership team and the COE initiate goals, projects, and tasks that move the organization toward the new vision and identify the roles employees will play in reaching it. When a proposed change will take multiple years to implement, the leadership team and COE identify milestones throughout the life of the project. These milestones are incremental goals with specific completion dates that ensure that the project stays on track.

The leadership team clearly communicates the required actions through published goals and team charters. When goals must be broken down into smaller actions assigned to different organizational units, the team communicates the relationship and relevance of the assigned actions to the overarching goal.

The milestones represent visible improvements or short-term accomplishments that are part of the progress toward the project goal. But rather than initiating one sweeping change throughout the organization, management may initiate changes on a smaller scale, such as in one department or division, and announce successes to the entire organization. For example, one goal could require the underwriting department to create a framework for using data mining to better evaluate products liability risks within six months. And because success in one department builds confidence in the change that can carry over to others, the leadership team celebrates the achievement of each milestone and rewards the people responsible.

Entrench the Change

As the organization achieves milestones, it must take steps to entrench its hard-earned progress and prevent regression. New behaviors must be sustained, and gains should be consolidated and anchored to the organization's culture through formal policies and structures. The organization's culture—the shared attitudes, values, goals, and persistent norms of behavior—must be aligned with the change to data-driven philosophies. Shared values based on the vision should persist throughout the systems, processes, and structures created.

Individuals may not be able to see the broader perspective or effect of the change while it is taking place. Once the change is completed, the leadership team and COE must articulate the connection between the new behaviors and processes and organizational success so that employees understand the scope of what has transpired and the positive outcome. New approaches will become part of the culture of the organization only when it is clear that they work and are superior to prior methods.

SUMMARY

A SWOT (strengths, weaknesses, opportunities, and threats) analysis focused specifically on the potential use of data analytics enables an insurer's management to examine internal (organizational) strengths and weaknesses that could potentially be affected by a data analytics initiative and external factors that present opportunities for growth or threats to the organization's survival.

Successfully managing risks in a data analytics project involves understanding the risk management process—scanning the environment, identifying risks, analyzing risks, treating risks, and monitoring and assuring the results—to identify, assess, and respond to risk appropriately.

An insurer's transition to a data-driven decision-making culture is initiated by a change agent and developed by a leadership team and a COE. The process involves all employees in an organization by building commitment to a common vision that fundamentally alters the way the organization operates. These are the change management steps:

1. Articulate the need for change
2. Appoint a leadership team
3. Develop a written statement of the vision and strategies
4. Communicate the vision and strategies
5. Eliminate barriers to change
6. Recognize incremental successes
7. Entrench the change

ASSIGNMENT NOTES

1. Kathryn M. Bartol and David C. Martin, Management, 3rd ed. (New York: McGraw-Hill Cos., Inc., 1998), p. 228.
2. Ari Chester, Richard Clarke, and Ari Libarikian, "Transforming Into an Analytics-Driven Insurance Carrier," McKinsey and Company, February 2016, www.mckinsey.com/industries/financial-services/our-insights/transforming-into-an-analytics-driven-insurance-carrier (accessed June 22, 2016).
3. Morag Cuddeford Jones, "How to Beat Your Competition Using Analytics in Insurance," FC Business Intelligence, 2015, www.the-digital-insurer.com/how-to-beat-your-competition-using-analytics-in-insurance-fc-business-intelligence-report-by-morag-cuddeford-jones/ (accessed June 22, 2016).

Index

Page numbers in boldface refer to pages where the word or phrase is defined.

P

Q

R

S

T

U

V

W